Digesting Jung

Marie-Louise von Franz, Honorary Patron

Studies in Jungian Psychology by Jungian Analysts

Daryl Sharp, General Editor

DIGESTING JUNG

Food for the Journey

DARYL SHARP

Daryl Sharp is the author of 11 other books in this Series.
See page 127 for details.

Canadian Cataloguing in Publication Data

Sharp, Daryl, 1936-
Digesting Jung: food for the journey

(Studies in Jungian psychology by Jungian analysts; 95)

Includes bibliographical references and index.

ISBN 0-919123-96-1

1. Jung, C.G. (Carl Gustav), 1875-1961.
2. Psychoanalysis.
I. Title. II. Series.

BF173.S518 2001 150.19'54 C00-933184-0

INNER CITY BOOKS
Box 1271, Station Q, Toronto, ON M4T 2P4, Canada
Telephone (416) 927-0355 / Fax (416) 924-1814
Web site: www.innercitybooks.net / E-mail: admin@innercitybooks.net

Honorary Patron: Marie-Louise von Franz.
Publisher and General Editor: Daryl Sharp.
Senior Editor: Victoria B. Cowan.

INNER CITY BOOKS was founded in 1980 to promote the understanding and practical application of the work of C.G. Jung.

Index by Vicki Cowan

Printed and bound in Canada by University of Toronto Press Incorporated

CONTENTS

See final page for descriptions of other Inner City Books

Preface

As a young man I had a burning ambition to be a writer. I have become one, but my lot in life has not been to be a novelist. Rather, following my own process of individuation, I have become nothing more nor less than a journeyman dedicated to promoting the understanding and practical application of Jung's work. That is my vocation, both as writer and publisher, and I am glad of it.

This particular book evolved out of a desire to pinpoint key passages in Jung's writings that have nourished me for many years. It provides readers new to analytical psychology with the main ingredients of Jung's work and how they might flavor a life. Those already familiar with Jung's ideas will savor again the continuing relevance of his holistic approach to psychological issues.

The appetizers that head each chapter are fleshed out by my commentaries—elucidations of Jung's ideas or experiential interpretations, sometimes both—meant to stimulate the reader to ruminate on what is happening in his or her own life and the unconscious factors that for good or ill influence the lives of each of us.

Those seeking a more robust meal will be amply rewarded by following up the footnote references.

* * *

The shoe that fits one person pinches another; there is no universal recipe for living. Each of us carries his own life-form within him—an irrational form which no other can outbid.[1]

[1] "The Aims of Psychotherapy," *The Practice of Psychotherapy,* CW 16, par. 81. (CW refers throughout to *The Collected Works of C.G. Jung)*

Jung in 1959, at the age of 84
(photo by Hugo Charteris)

1
It's a Complex Life

Everyone knows nowadays that people "have complexes." What is not so well known, though far more important theoretically, is that complexes can have us.[2]

We like to think we are masters in our own house, but clearly we are not. We are renters at best. Psychologically we live in a boarding house of saints and knaves, nobles and villains, run by a landlord who for all we know is indifferent to the lot. We fancy we can do what we want, but when it comes to a showdown our will is hampered by fellow boarders with a mind of their own.

In the jargon of Jungian psychology, these "fellow boarders" are known as complexes.

Just as atoms and molecules are the invisible components of physical objects, complexes are the building blocks of the psyche. Complexes in themselves are not negative, but their effects often are, for they determine our emotional reactions.

When I first went into analysis I knew nothing about complexes. I knew only that I was at the end of my rope, on my knees. Then I took Jung's Word Association Experiment, a test he developed almost a century ago to illustrate how unconscious factors can disturb the workings of consciousness. It is the precursor of the modern lie detector test, though rather more revealing in its broader scope.

In the Word Association Experiment an examiner reads from a list of a hundred words, to each of which you are asked to respond with what first comes into your head. The delay in responding (the response time) is measured with a stop watch.

Here is how it goes:

---

[2] "A Review of the Complex Theory," *The Structure and Dynamics of the Psyche,* CW 8, par. 200.

"Head"— "bed" (0.8 sec.)
"Marry"— "together" (1.7 sec.)
"Woman"— "friend" (2 sec.)
"Home"—(long pause) "none" (5.6 sec.)

—and so on.

Then the examiner takes you through the list a second time, noting different responses to the same words. Finally you are asked for comments on those words to which you had a longer-than-average response time, a merely mechanical response or a different association on the second run-through. All these had been flagged by the examiner as "complex indicators."

My experience of the Word Association Experiment was both illuminating and deflating. It convinced me that complexes were not only real but were alive in me and quite autonomous, independent of my will. I realized they could affect my memory, my thoughts, my moods, my behavior. I was not free to be me—there *was* no "me"—when I was in the grip of a complex.

Freud described dreams as the *via regia* to the unconscious; Jung showed that the royal road to the unconscious is rather the complex, the architect of both dreams and symptoms. In fact, Jung originally gave the name "complex psychology" to his school of thought, to distinguish it from Freud's school of psychoanalysis.

The activation of a complex is always marked by the presence of some strong emotion, be it love or hate, joy or anger, or any other. We are all complexed by something, which is to say, we all react emotionally when the right buttons are pushed. Or, to put it another way, an emotional reaction *means* that a complex has been constellated. When a complex is activated we can't think straight and hardly know how we feel. We speak and act according to the dictates of the complex, and when it has run its course we wonder what took over.

We cannot get rid of our complexes, simply because they are deeply rooted in our personal history. Complexes are part and parcel of who we are. The most we can do is become aware of how we are influenced by them and how they interfere with our conscious intentions. As long as we are unconscious of our complexes, we are prone to being overwhelmed or driven by them. When we understand them, they lose their power to affect us. They do not disappear, but over time their grip on us can loosen.

A complex is a bundle of associations, sometimes painful, sometimes joyful, always accompanied by affect. It has energy and a life of its own. It can upset digestion, breathing and the rate at which the heart beats. It behaves like a partial personality. When we want to say or do something and a complex interferes, we find ourselves saying or doing something quite different from what we intended. Our best intentions are upset, exactly as if we had been interfered with by another person.

Complexes can take over to such an extent that they become visible and audible. They appear as visions and speak in voices that are like those of definite people. This is not necessarily a pathological symptom (e.g., schizophrenia). Complexes are regularly personified in dreams, and one can train oneself so they become visible or audible also in a waking condition, as in the practice of active imagination.[3] It is even psychologically healthy to do so, for when you give them a voice, a face, a personality, they are less likely to take over when you're not looking.

The existence of complexes goes a long way toward explaining both multiple personality disorders and what the helping professions call lost memory recovery. An early trauma is often at the root of such cases. What may happen in response to a painful traumatic event is that the ego dissociates. The self-regulating function of the psyche is activated and creates a complex that dis-remembers the event—it gets buried among the detritus of ongoing life.[4] Like any other complex, it lies dogg-o in the unconscious until something happens to trigger it.

---

[3] See below, pp. 106ff.

[4] See below, pp. 55ff., for commentary on the self-regulating function of the psyche, a keynote belief in the practice of Jungian analysis.

Over the past hundred years the word "complex" has become common currency, but what it means, and the effects complexes have on our lives, are not so widely understood. This is unfortunate, for until we realize that, as Jung says, "complexes can have us," we are doomed to live a life forever hampered by them, forever ruled by inner forces, forever at odds with others.

2
Complex, Archetype and Instinct

[Archetypes] are, indeed, an instinctive trend, *as marked as the impulse of birds to build nests, or ants to form organized colonies.*[5]

At the core of any personal complex there is an archetype. For instance, behind emotional associations with the personal mother (that is, the mother complex), there is the archetype of the mother—an age-old collective image spanning humanity's experience of mothering, from nourishment and security ("positive" mother) to devouring possessiveness ("negative" mother). Similarly, behind the father complex there is the father archetype—all the experienced diversity of fathering down through the ages, from authoritarian to permissive and all shades between.

Jung's concept of archetypes undercuts the naive notion that human beings are born into the world *tabula rasa,* a blank slate waiting to be writ upon by life. He comments:

> Archetypes are systems of readiness for action, and at the same time images and emotions. They are inherited with the brain structure—indeed they are its psychic aspect.[6]
>
> It is not . . . a question of inherited *ideas* but of inherited *possibilities* of ideas. Nor are they individual acquisitions but, in the main, common to all, as can be seen from [their] universal occurrence.[7]
>
> Archetypes . . . present themselves *as ideas and images,* like everything else that becomes a content of consciousness.[8]

---

[5] Jung, "Approaching the Unconscious," in *Man and His Symbols,* p. 69.
[6] "Mind and Earth," *Civilization in Transition,* CW 10, par. 53.
[7] "Concerning the Archetypes and the Anima Concept," *The Archetypes and the Collective Unconscious,* CW 9i, par. 136.
[8] "On the Nature of the Psyche," *The Structure and Dynamics of the Psyche,* CW 8, par. 435.

Archetypes are not knowable in themselves, but their myriad manifestations—as images, patterns and motifs—are well documented in art, literature, history and mythology. Odysseus, Joan of Arc and Pinocchio are archetypal images of the hero archetype; the goddess Demeter is an archetypal image of the mother archetype; the gods Saturn and Zeus are archetypal images of the father; Satan is a personified image of the archetype of evil; political parties on right and left act out the "two brothers" motif (as in the enmity of Cain and Abel), and so on. Needless to say, the names given to archetypal patterns differ according to the prevailing culture.

Jung used the simile of the spectrum to illustrate the difference between instinct and the archetype as an "instinctual image":

> The dynamism of instinct is lodged as it were in the infra-red part of the spectrum, whereas the instinctual image lies in the ultra-violet part. . . . The realization and assimilation of instinct never take place at the red end, i.e., by absorption into the instinctual sphere, but only through integration of the image which signifies and at the same time evokes the instinct.[9]

Here is how he pictured the relationship between instinct and archetype, and the ways in which each may manifest:

INSTINCTS	**ARCHETYPES**
infrared ————————————	———————————— ultraviolet
(**Physiological:** body symptoms, instinctual perceptions, etc.)	(**Psychological:** spirit, dreams, conceptions, images, fantasies, etc.)

So, an archetype is a primordial, structural element of the human psyche—a universal tendency to form certain ideas and images and to behave in certain ways. Instincts are the physiological counterparts of archetypes. Complexes, arising from our individual experience in the here and now, put skin and flesh on the collective bones of instinct, archetype and archetypal image.

---

[9] Ibid., par. 414.

In the process of attending to images in my dreams, and tracking my daily emotional reactions to others, I have developed a deep belief in the existence of complexes, a respectful attitude toward my own, and a wonderment for what is behind them.

Others may attribute what happens in their lives to the guiding hand of God, or chance, fate, the alignment of planets, whatever. I prefer Jung's theory of archetypes, from which follows the personal responsibility to become conscious of how they manifest in one's day-to-day life.

3
A Psychological Compass

The four functions are somewhat like the four points of the compass; they are just as arbitrary and just as indispensable. . . . But one thing I must confess: I would not for anything dispense with this compass on my psychological voyages of discovery.[10]

Why do we move through life the way we do? Why are we better at some activities than others? Why do some of us prefer to be alone rather than with other people—or at a party instead of reading a book? Why don't we all function in the same way?

From earliest times, attempts have been made to categorize individual attitudes and behavior patterns in order to explain the differences between people. Jung's model of typology is one of them. It is the basis for modern "tests" such as the Myers-Briggs Type Indicator (MBTI), used by corporations and institutions in order to classify a person's interests, attitudes and behavior patterns, and hence the type of work or education they might be best suited for.

Jung did not develop his model of psychological types for this purpose. Rather than label people as this or that type, he sought simply to explain the differences between the ways we function and interact with our surroundings in order to promote a better understanding of human psychology in general, and one's own way of seeing the world in particular.

After extensive years research, Jung identified eight typological groups: two personality attitudes—*introversion* and *extraversion*—and four functions—*thinking, sensation, intuition* and *feeling,* each of which may operate in an introverted or extraverted way.

In Jung's model, introversion and extraversion are psychological modes of adaptation. In the former, the movement of energy is to-

---

[10] "A Psychological Theory of Types," *Psychological Types,* CW 6, pars. 958f.

ward the inner world. In the latter, interest is directed toward the outer world. In one case the subject (inner reality) and in the other the object (outer reality) is of primary importance. Whether one is predominately introverted or extraverted—as opposed to what one is doing at any particular time—depends on the direction one's energy naturally, and usually, flows.[11]

Each of the four functions has its special area of expertise. *Thinking* refers to the process of cognitive thought; *sensation* is perception by means of the physical sense organs; *feeling* is the function of subjective judgment or valuation; and *intuition* refers to perception via the unconscious.

Briefly, the sensation function establishes that something exists, thinking tells us what it means, feeling tells us what it's worth to us, and through intuition we have a sense of what can be done with it (the possibilities).

No one function by itself (and neither attitude alone) is sufficient for ordering our experience of ourselves or the world around us:

> For complete orientation all four functions should contribute equally: thinking should facilitate cognition and judgment, feeling should tell us how and to what extent a thing is important or unimportant for us, sensation should convey concrete reality to us through seeing, hearing, tasting, etc., and intuition should enable us to divine the hidden possibilities in the background, since these too belong to the complete picture of a given situation.[12]

In everyday usage, the feeling function is often confused with an emotional reaction. Emotion, more properly called affect, is invariably the result of an activated complex, which is accompanied by noticeable physical symptoms. When not contaminated by a

---

[11] Note that introversion is quite different from introspection, which refers to self-examination. Although introverts may have more time or inclination for introspection than do extraverts, introverts have no monopoly on psychological awareness.

[12] Ibid., par. 900. Jung acknowledged that the four orienting functions do not contain everything in the conscious psyche. Will power and memory, for instance, are not included in his model, because although they may be affected by the way one functions typologically, they are not in themselves typological determinants.

complex, feeling can in fact be quite cold.

Jung's basic model, including the relationship between the four functions, is a quaternity. In the following diagram, thinking is arbitrarily placed at the top; any of the other functions might be put there, according to which one a person most favors.

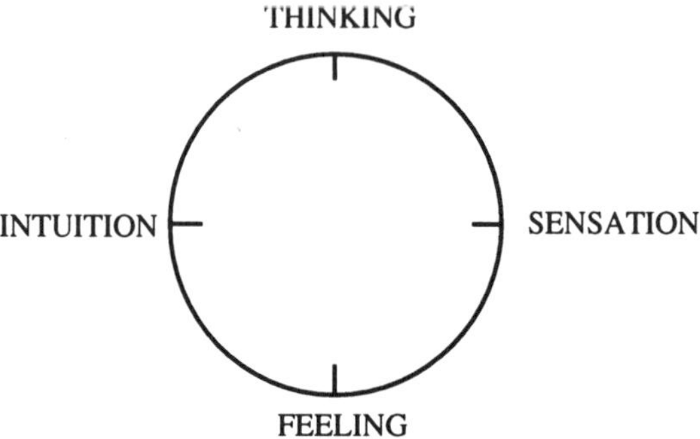

Typologically, opposites can attract or repel. Hence it is common for someone with a dominant thinking function, for instance, to be attracted to a feeling type—or shun such a person because of his or her very differentness. Similarly, intuitives may be drawn to, or distance themselves from, those with a good sensation function, and vice versa. A better understanding of these opposites—latent or dormant in ourselves—can mitigate such reactions, which often have little or nothing to do with the reality of the other person.

To my mind, Jung's model is most helpful when it is used not as a way to classify oneself or others, but rather in the way he originally thought of it, as a psychological compass. So, in any problematic situation, I ask myself four questions:

1) What are the facts? (sensation)
2) Have I thought it through? (thinking)
3) What is it worth to me to pursue this? (feeling)
4) What are the possibilities? (intuition)

The answers aren't always clear, but the questions keep me on my toes. That is by and large why I don't favor type tests. Type tests concretize what is inherently variable, and thereby overlook the dynamic nature of the psyche.

Any system of typology is no more than a gross indicator of what people have in common and the differences between them. Jung's model is no exception. It is distinguished solely by its parameters—the two attitudes and the four functions. What it does not and cannot show, nor does it pretend to, is the uniqueness of the individual. Also, no one is a pure type. It would be foolish to even try to reduce an individual personality to this or that, just one thing or another. Each of us is a conglomeration, an admixture of attitudes and functions that in their combination defy classification. All that is true, and emphatically acknowledged by Jung—

> One can never give a description of a type, no matter how complete, that would apply to more than one individual, despite the fact that in some ways it aptly characterizes thousands of others. Conformity is one side of a man, uniqueness is the other.[13]

—but it does not obviate the practical value of his model, particularly when one has run aground on the shoals of his or her own psychology.

Whether Jung's model is "true" or not—objectively true—is a moot point. Indeed, is anything ever "objectively" true? The real truth is that Jung's model of psychological types has all the advantages and disadvantages of any scientific model. Although lacking statistical verification, it is equally hard to disprove. But it accords with experiential reality. Moreover, since it is based on a fourfold—mandala-like—way of looking at things that is archetypal, it is *psychologically satisfying.*

As mentioned earlier, one's behavior can be quite misleading in determining typology. For instance, to enjoy being with other people is characteristic of the extraverted attitude, but this does not automatically mean that a person who enjoys lots of company is an extraverted type. Naturally, one's activities will to some extent be

---

[13] *Psychological Types,* CW 6, par. 895.

determined by typology, but the interpretation of those activities in terms of typology depends on the value system behind the action. Where the subject—oneself—and a personal value system are the dominant motivating factors, there is by definition an introverted type, whether at a party or alone. Similarly, when one is predominantly oriented to the object—things and other people—there is an extraverted type, whether in a crowd or on one's own. This is what makes Jung's system primarily a model of *personality* rather than of behavior.

Everything psychic is relative. I cannot say, think or do anything that is not colored by my particular way of seeing the world, which in turn is a manifestation of both my typology and my complexes. This psychological rule is analogous to Einstein's famous theory of relativity in physics, and equally as significant.

Being aware of the way I tend to function makes it possible for me to assess my attitudes and behavior in a given situation and adjust them accordingly. It enables me both to compensate for my personal disposition and to be tolerant of someone who does not function as I do—someone who has, perhaps, a strength or facility I myself lack.

Typologically speaking, the important question is not whether one is innately introverted or extraverted, or which function is superior or inferior, but, more pragmatically: in *this* situation, with *that* person, how did I function and with what effect? Did my actions truly reflect my judgments (thinking and feeling) and perceptions (sensation and intuition)? And if not, why not? What complexes were activated in me? To what end? How and why did I mess things up? What does this say about my psychology? What can I do about it? What do I *want* to do about it?

These are among the questions we must take to heart if we want to be psychologically conscious.

4
Who Are We, Really?

The persona is that which in reality one is not,
but which oneself as well as others think one is.[14]

We have a name, perhaps a title, perform a function in the outside world. We are this, that or the other. To some extent all this is real, yet in relation to our essential individuality, what we seem to be is only a secondary, superficial reality.

Jung describes the persona as an aspect of the collective psyche, which means there is nothing individual about it. It may *feel* individual—quite special and unique, in fact—but our persona is on the one hand simply a social identity, and on the other an ideal image of ourselves.

Like any other complex, one's persona has certain attributes and behavior patterns associated with it, as well as collective expectations to live up to: a struggling writer, for instance, is a serious thinker, on the brink of recognition; a teacher is a figure of authority, dedicated to imparting knowledge; a doctor is wise, versed in the arcane mysteries of the body; a priest is close to God, morally impeccable; a mother loves her children and would sacrifice her life for them; an accountant knows his figures but is unemotional, and so on.

That is why we experience a sense of shock when we read of a teacher accused of molesting a student, a doctor charged with drug abuse, a priest on the hook for pedophilia, a mother who breaks her children's bones, or kills them; an accountant who fiddles the books; a pillar of the community caught with his pants down.

The development of a collectively suitable persona always in-

[14] "Concerning Rebirth," *The Archetypes and the Collective Unconscious,* CW 9i, par. 221.

volves a compromise between what we know ourselves to be and what is expected of us, such as a degree of courtesy and innocuous behavior. There is nothing intrinsically wrong with that. In Greek, the word *persona* meant a mask worn by actors to indicate the role they played. On this level, it is an asset in mixing with other people. It is also useful as a protective covering. Close friends may know us for what we are; the rest of the world knows only what we choose to show them. Indeed, without an outer layer of some kind, we are simply too vulnerable. Only the foolish and naive attempt to move through life without a persona.

However, we must be able to drop our persona in situations where it is not appropriate. This is especially true in intimate relationships. There is a difference between myself as an analyst and who I am when I'm not practicing. The doctor's professional bedside manner is little comfort to a neglected mate. The teacher's credentials do not impress her teenage son who wants to borrow the car. The wise preacher leaves his collar and his rhetoric at home when he goes courting.

By handsomely rewarding the persona, the outside world invites us to identify with it. Money, respect and power come to those who can perform single-mindedly and well in a social role. No wonder we can forget that our essential identity is something other than the work we do, our function in the collective. From being a useful convenience, therefore, the persona easily becomes a trap. It is one thing to realize this, but quite another to do something about it.

The poet Rainer Maria Rilke put it quite well:

> We discover, indeed, that we do not know our part; we look for a mirror; we want to rub off the paint, to remove all that is artificial and become real. But somewhere a bit of mummery that we forget still sticks to us. A trace of exaggeration remains in our eyebrows; we do not notice that the corners of our lips are twisted. And thus we go about, a laughing-stock, a mere half-thing: neither real beings nor actors.[15]

[15] *The Notebook of Malte Laurids Brigge,* p. 217.

Identification with a social role is a frequent source of midlife crisis. This is so because it inhibits our adaptation to a given situation beyond what is collectively prescribed. Who am I without a mask? Is there anybody home? I am a prominent and respected member of the community. Why, then, is my wife interested in someone else?

Many married people cultivate a joint persona as "a happy couple." Whatever may be happening between them, they greet the world with a united front. They are perfectly matched, the envy of their friends. What goes on behind the curtains is anybody's guess, and nobody's else's business, for sure, but how many "happy couples" feel trapped in their persona and stay together simply because they don't know who they are alone?

We cannot get rid of ourselves in favor of a collective identity without some consequences. We lose sight of who we are without our protective covering; our reactions are predetermined by collective expectations (we do and think and feel what our persona "should" do, think and feel); erratic moods betray our real feelings; those close to us complain of our emotional distance; and, worst of all, we cannot imagine life without it.

Assuming we recognize the problem, and suffer because of it, what are we to do about it? Personal analysis is a possibility for those who can afford it. Otherwise, some reading in the literature of depth psychology would not go amiss. But avoid "quick-fix" books, confessional memoirs by those who would seduce you into imitating them. Your task is to discover who *you* are.

Here are some tips:

1) Pay attention to your dreams; mull over their content, and don't think you have to "understand" them to get the message.

2) Monitor your feelings in both intimate and social situations.

3) Become aware of how and when you use your persona for legitimate reasons, and when you are simply hiding behind it.

4) Think about what it means to lead an authentic life.

5
Shadow Boxing

The shadow is a moral problem that challenges the whole ego-personality . . . . To become conscious of it involves recognizing the dark aspects of the personality as present and real.[16]

To the degree that we identify with a bright and blameless persona, our shadow is correspondingly dark. The persona aims at perfection. The shadow reminds us we are human.

Everything about ourselves that we are not conscious of is shadow. Psychologically, the shadow opposes and compensates the persona, the "I" we show to the outside world. Where we are concerned to put on a good front, to do what is considered by others to be proper, our shadow is not. The realization of how and when our shadow enters our life, and at times takes over, is a precondition for self-knowledge. The more we become conscious of our shadow's intentions and behavior, the less of a threat it is and the more psychologically substantial we become.

In Jung's description, the shadow, or at least its dark side, is composed of morally inferior wishes and motives, childish fantasies and resentments, etc.—all those things about ourselves we are not proud of and regularly seek to hide from others. For instance, in civilized societies aggression is a prominent aspect of the shadow, simply because it is not socially acceptable; it is nipped in the bud in childhood and its expression in adult life is met with heavy sanctions. The same is true of sexual behavior that deviates from the collective norm.

By and large, then, the shadow is a hodge-podge of repressed desires and "uncivilized" impulses. It is possible to become conscious of these, but in the meantime they are projected onto others.

[16] "The Shadow," *Aion,* CW 9ii, par. 14.

Just as we may mistake a real man or woman for the soul-mate we yearn for, so we see our devils, our shadow, in others. This is responsible for much acrimony in personal relationships. On a collective level it gives rise to political polarization, wars and the ubiquitous practice of scapegoating.

Realizing our shadow is not easy because we tend to cling to our persona, the ideal image we have of ourselves, which in a culture based on Judeo-Christian values is heavily influenced by the thou-shalt-nots enshrined in the Ten Commandments.

In everyday life, we do many things under the influence of a shadow fed up with the persona. We cheat on our tax returns; we lie, steal, kill and sleep with our neighbor's wife. When called to account, we are shamefaced and wonder who did it.

There is no generally effective way to assimilate the shadow. It is more like diplomacy or statesmanship, and it is always an individual matter. Shadow and ego are like two political parties jockeying for power. If one can speak of a technique at all, it consists solely in an attitude.

First, one has to accept and take seriously the existence of the shadow. You do this by taking note of how others react to you and you to them. Second, one has to become aware of the shadow's qualities and intentions. You discover this through conscientious attention to moods, fantasies and impulses. (Best to write them down, for future reference.) Third, a lengthy process of negotiation between you-as-you'd-like-to-be and you-as-you'd-rather-not-be is unavoidable.

On the other hand, the shadow is not only the dark underside of the conscious personality. It also has a bright side: aspects of ourselves that comprise our unlived life—talents and abilities that have long been buried or never been conscious; part and parcel of who we are meant to be. They are potentially available, and their conscious realization often releases a surprising amount of energy.

That is why, in Jungian analysis, a depressed or fearful person is counseled to go into their fear or depression rather than try to escape it. "Going into" a mood means confronting it. Don't identify with it; rather, give it a name and dialogue with it. The buried treasure in our moods can only be unearthed by conscious effort.

Personally, in dialoguing with any particular shadow inclination of my own, I find it helpful, in deciding whether or not to act it out, to have at least these questions in mind :

1) Is it legal?
2) Could it endanger my life?
3) How might it affect my loved ones?
4) Could I live with the consequences?

A psychological crisis activates both sides of the shadow: those qualities and activities we are not proud of, and possibilities we never knew or have forgotten were there. Associated with the former—according to consciously-held moral values—is a sense of shame and distaste. The latter may have morally neutral connotations, but they are often more frightening because if we follow up on our latent possibilities there is no telling what might happen.

In practice, ego and shadow can either collaborate or tear each other apart. This is a powerful and widespread archetypal motif. It is found in the Biblical stories of Cain and Abel, Isaac and Ishmael, Jacob and Esau; in Egyptian mythology there is Horus and Set; in Christianity, Yahweh and Satan, Christ and Judas. In Freudian terminology it is known as sibling rivalry. In Jungian psychology it is called the hostile brothers motif.

One of the world's oldest surviving myths, the Gilgamesh Epic, exemplifies this motif. It illustrates not only the initial conflict between an inflated ego and an instinctual shadow—a conflict we must all come to grips with in order to have a balanced personality—but also their cooperative triumphs and what can happen when one loses the other. The story of Gilgamesh was laboriously chiseled in stone tablets some seven thousand years ago. Briefly, it goes like this:

Gilgamesh was a young Sumerian ruler, half man and half god, who after many heroic exploits became proud and arrogant. Seeing Gilgamesh's tyranny over his subjects, the gods sent down a brother, Enkidu, to teach him a lesson. Enkidu was an animal-man. His whole body was covered with hair. At first he roamed wild on the plains, living close to nature. He was all animal until a woman dragged him into the bush and tore off his pelt. Then he became half man, familiar with lust, and ravaged the countryside.

Gilgamesh was angered by news of Enkidu and challenged him to do battle. Enkidu accepted and they tangled at the temple gates. It was a long and nasty struggle. They fought tooth and nail, but in the end it was a stand-off. They then embraced and toasted each other as best friends.

Together, Gilgamesh and Enkidu were half man, a quarter god and a quarter animal. For years thereafter they traveled the world righting wrongs, defeating awesome monsters like Humbaba, guardian of the cedar forest, and the bull of heaven, a fearsome beast created by the gods to destroy Gilgamesh because he refused the advances of the goddess Ishtar.

Then Enkidu became sick and died. That was the decree of the gods, to placate Ishtar for Gilgamesh's rejection of her.

Gilgamesh was bereft. He set out on a quest for the elixir of life. After a long journey he finally he found it in the shape of a thorny plant at the bottom of the sea. Joyfully he set off for home. But one day, as he was taking a cold bath in a clear pond, a snake crept into his camp and ate the plant. Gilgamesh gnashed his teeth and wept bitterly. He had had the elixir of life in hand and he lost it! He died a broken man.

Thus, according to the legend, snakes gained the power to shed their old skin and thereby renew their life. We humans still have to do it the hard way.

6
Reality As We Know It

All the contents of our unconscious are constantly being projected into our surroundings, and it is only by recognizing certain properties of the objects as projections or imagos that we are able to distinguish them from the real properties of the objects.[17]

Willy-nilly, we see our own unacknowledged mistakes and blind-spots in others. This is abundantly clear in personal quarrels and in politics. Without an unusual degree of self-awareness we seldom see through our projections; but if we do not we will be victimized by them.

Our human nature inclines us to believe that the world is as we see it, that people are who we imagine them to be. However, other people frequently turn out to be completely different from the way we thought they were. If they are not particularly close, we think no more about it. If such an experience involves one of our intimates, we are rather more concerned and in some cases devastated.

Jung was among the first to point out that we see unacknowledged aspects of ourselves in other people. In so doing, we create a series of imaginary relationships that often have little or nothing to do with the persons we relate to. This is quite normal, a just-so story of life. However, psychological maturity depends in no small part on becoming aware of when, how and why we project.

Projection has generally had a bad press, but in its positive sense it creates an agreeable bridge between people, facilitating friendship and communication. Like the persona, projection greases the wheels of social intercourse. And as with complexes, life would be a lot duller without it.

There is passive projection and there is active projection. Passive

---

[17] "General Aspects of Dream Psychology," *The Archetypes and the Collective Unconscious,* CW 9i, par. 507.

projection is completely automatic and unintentional. Our eyes catch another's across a crowded room and we are smitten, head over heels. Or we are immediately repelled by what we "see." We may know nothing about that person; in fact the less we know the easier it is to project. We fill the void with ourselves. Active projection, also called empathy, occurs when you feel yourself into the other's shoes by imagining what he or she is going through. This is a positive concomitant of most close friendships.

There is a thin line between empathy and identification. Identification presupposes no separation between subject and object, no difference between me and the other person. We are two peas in a pod. What is good for me must be good for him—or her. Many relationships run aground on this mistaken notion. It is the motivation for much well-meaning advice to others, and the premise of any therapeutic system relying on suggestion or adaptation to collectively sanctioned behavior and ideals.

In close relationships, identification is as common as potatoes. When you identify with another person, your emotional well-being is intimately linked with the mood of that person and his or her attitude toward you. Neither can make a move without double-thinking the effect on the other, which automatically inhibits the self-expression of both. Such a relationship is psychologically no different from that between parent and child, nor is it easy to tell, at any given time, who is parent and who is child.

Projection, if it doesn't go as far as identification, is actually quite useful in terms of self-knowledge. When we assume something about another person and then discover this to be an illusion, we are obliged to realize that the world and those in it are not our own creation. If we are reflective, we can learn something about ourselves. This is called withdrawing projections—bringing them home, so to speak.

A common example of projection is that of a husband or wife who suspects the other of an illicit affair. Of course this may be a true perception, but if it is unfounded in reality it may be that the suspicious mate actually has an unconscious desire for another partner, which secret wish is projected onto the other.

On the whole, it only becomes necessary to withdraw projections when our expectations of others are frustrated. If there is no obvious disparity between what we expect, or imagine to be true, and the reality we experience, then there is no need to speak of projection at all. Let sleeping dogs lie, as long as they will.

Also on the positive side, it must be said that projection can constellate unrealized or dormant qualities in another person. Parental expectations notoriously lead one astray, but they can also be the stimulus to explore one's potential. Many a grown man or woman owes his or her accomplishments to the urgings of a prescient friend or lover. As long as power over the other, or the projection of one's own unlived life, is not lurking in the shadows, no harm is done. Indeed, in such cases it is better to speak not of projection but of genuine human relationship.

Where love reigns, there is no will to power; and where the will to power is paramount, love is lacking.[18]

---

[18] *Two Essays on Analytic Psychology,* CW 7, par. 78.

7
Typology Revisited

The superior function is always an expression of the conscious personality, of its aims, will, and general performance, whereas the less differentiated functions fall into the category of things that simply "happen" to one.[19]

Over the years, Jung's model of typology, outlined here earlier, has been very significant to me as a psychological compass. But I have to say that I learned almost as much about typology from living with Arnold as I did from reading Jung.

I met Arnold only a few weeks before leaving for Zurich, where we had both been accepted to train at the Jung Institute. We took to each other and agreed to share a place, which I offered to find since I would be there first. I house-hunted for a week and found a gem.

Arnold, it turned out, was a raving intuitive. I met him at the station when he arrived. It was the third train I'd met. True to his type, his letter had been sketchy on details. True to my predominantly sensation orientation, I wasn't.

"I've rented an old house in the country," I told him, hefting his bag. The lock was broken and the straps were gone. One wheel was missing. "Twelve and a half minutes on the train and it's never late. The house has green shutters and polka-dot wallpaper. The garden is bursting with forsythia, roses, clematis and lily of the valley. The landlady is a Swiss businesswoman from the Engadine, an attractive blond. She says we can furnish it the way we want."

"Great!" said Arnold, holding a newspaper over his head. It was pouring out. He had no hat and he'd forgotten to bring his raincoat. He was wearing slippers, for God's sake. We couldn't find his trunk because he'd booked it through to Lucerne.

---

[19] "General Description of the Types," *Psychological Types*, CW 6, par. 575.

"Lucerne, Zurich, it's all Switzerland to me," he shrugged.

It was quite amusing at first. I'd never been close to anyone quite so . . . well, so *different.*

Time meant nothing to Arnold. He missed trains, he missed appointments. He was always late for class, and when he finally found the right room he didn't have anything to write with. He didn't know a budget from a budgie; he either had bags of money or none at all. He didn't know east from west, he got lost whenever he left the house. And sometimes in it.

"You need a seeing-eye dog," I joked.

"Not as long as you're around," he grinned.

He left the stove on overnight. He never turned out lights. Pots boiled over, meat turned black, while he sat on the porch watching the sky and musing. The kitchen was forever filled with the smell of burnt toast. He lost his keys, his wallet, his lecture notes, his passport. He never had a clean shirt. In his old leather jacket, baggy jeans and two different socks he looked like a bum.

His room was always a mess, like a hurricane had hit.

"It drives me crazy just to look at you," I hummed, adjusting my tie in the mirror.

I liked to be neatly turned out, it made me feel good. I knew precisely where everything was. My desk was ordered, my room was always tidy. I turned out the lights when I left the house and I had an excellent sense of direction. I didn't lose anything and I was always on time. I could cook and I could sew. I knew exactly how much money was in my pocket. Nothing escaped me, I remembered all the details.

"You don't live in the real world," I observed, as Arnold set out to fry an egg. A real hero's journey. He couldn't find the frying pan and when he did he put it on the cold burner.

"Reality as *you* know it," he said, quite hurt.

"Damn!" he cursed. He'd burnt himself again.

I need not say much here about the added aggravations due to Arnold being an extravert and me an introvert. Enough to say there were plenty. He brought people home at all hours of the day and night. I liked privacy, my own quiet space. I was concerned to keep to my timetable. During the day I escaped to my room and studied, or pretended to. At night I lay in bed with a pillow over my head, listening to them carouse.

On the other hand, Arnold's way of functioning was sometimes quite helpful. Like when we furnished the house.

Our landlady, Gretchen, took an immediate fancy to Arnold. God knows why, he didn't present as well as I did. "Just pick out what you want," she said. "You do the shopping, I'll pay the bills."

I had a few things in mind. So did Arnold. My ideas were quite modest, Arnold's were not. We already had beds and a few chairs. "A nice comfortable sofa," I said, as we entered the department store. "A bookcase and a desk for each of us, a couple of lamps. That's all we need."

"You have no imagination," said Arnold, steering me to the antiques. "You do the talking."

Naturally. I had not come to Switzerland without learning some German. Before leaving Canada I took a Berlitz course for six months. I wasn't fluent but I could make myself understood. I could also get by in French. Arnold knew no French and could not even count in German. I think he did not realize he was coming to a foreign country. I scolded him about this more than once.

"A few phrases," I implored. "Try saying hello, *Guten Tag.*"

"Aw," he said, "they all speak English."

As it turned out, they didn't. Worse, and to my chagrin, the language of the streets was Swiss German, a dialect, almost as different from German as Welsh or Scottish is from English. I was just about as helpless as Arnold.

Back to the department store. In one language or another, we managed to spend a lot of our landlady's money. While I fumbled to say exactly what I meant, Arnold waved his hands and gesticulated. By the time we left, ushered out by a grateful crowd of salespeople, we had a few things I hadn't thought of: a Chinese screen, two Indian carpets, a complete set of dishes and cutlery (for eight), ten pounds of bratwurst, a commode reputedly used by Louis XIV, and several numbered prints by Miro and Chagall.

Gretchen was thrilled. She gave us a special dinner. Arnold stayed behind when I left. "I'll just wrap up the lease," he winked.

I struggled to appreciate Arnold. I wanted to. His outgoing nature and natural ebullience were charming. I admired his air of careless confidence. He was the life of every party. He easily adapted to new situations. He was a lot more adventurous than I was. Where I hung back, tentative and wary, he plowed ahead. He easily made friends. And then brought them home.

He had an uncanny sense of perception. Whenever I got in a rut, bogged down in routine, he had something to suggest. His mind was fertile; it seethed with plans and new ideas. His hunches were usually right. It was like he had a sixth sense, while I was restricted to the usual five. My vision was mundane—where I saw a "thing" or a "person," Arnold saw, well, its soul.

But problems constantly arose between us. When he expressed an intention to do something I took him at his word. I believed he would do what he said he would. This was particularly annoying when we had arranged to meet at a certain time and place and he didn't show up.

"Look," I'd say, "I counted on you being there. I bought the tickets. Where were you?"

"I got waylaid," he'd counter defensively, "something else turned up, I couldn't resist."

"You're unstable, I can't depend on you. You're irresponsible and flighty. Why, you don't have a standpoint at all."

That isn't how Arnold saw it.

"I only express possibilities," he said, when for about the tenth time I accused him of being a social menace. "They aren't real until I say them, and when I do they take on some shape. But that doesn't mean I'll follow up on them. Something better might occur to me. I'm not tied to what I say. I can't help it if you take everything so damned literally."

He went on: "Intuitions are like birds circling in my head. They come and they go. I may not go with them, I never know, but I need time to authenticate their flight."

That was typical. I was prosaic, he was lyrical.

One morning I got up to find yet another pot boiled empty on a hot burner. Arnold struggled out of bed, looking for his glasses.

"Have you seen my razor?" he called.

"God damn it!" I shouted, furious, grabbing an oven mitt, "one day you'll burn down the house, we'll both be cinders. 'Alas,' they'll say, scooping our remains into little jars to send back to our loved ones, 'they had such potential. Too bad one of them was such a klutz!' "

Arnold shuffled into the kitchen as I threw the pot out the door.

"Oh yeah?" he said. "You made dinner last night for Cynthia, I wasn't even here."

It was true. My face got red. My balloon had been pricked. Reality as I knew it just got bigger.

"I forgot," I said meekly.

Arnold clapped his hands and danced around the room. "Join the human race!" he sang. As usual, he couldn't hold a note.

Only then did I realize that Arnold was my shadow. This was a revelation. It shouldn't have been, since we had already established that our complexes were radically different, but it struck me like a thunderbolt. I said as much to Arnold.

"You goof," he said. "You're my shadow as well. That's why you drive me up the wall."

We embraced.

All that was a long time ago. In the intervening years I've become more like Arnold. And he, more like me. Not only can he tell left from right now, he irons his tee-shirts and has learned to crochet. He dresses impeccably and his attention to detail is often sharper than mine. He lives alone and has a fabulous garden. He knows the names of all the flowers, in Latin.

Meanwhile, I have dinner parties and have been known to haunt the bars till dawn. I misplace precious papers. I forget names and telephone numbers. I can no longer find my way around a strange city. I pursue possibilities while things-to-do pile up around me. I could not cope without a cleaning lady.

Such developments are the unexpected consequences of getting to know your shadow and incorporating it in your life. You lose something of what you were, but you add a dimension that wasn't there before. Where you were one-sided, you find a balance. You learn to appreciate those who function differently and you develop a new attitude toward yourself.

Arnold and I are still shadow brothers, but now the tables are turned.

I tell him about my latest escapade. He shakes his head. "You damn gadabout," he says, punching my shoulder.

Arnold describes quiet evenings by the fire with a few intimate friends and says he never wants to travel again. This man, this great oaf, who used to be off and running at the drop of a hat.

"You're dull and predictable," I remark, cuffing him.

8
The Value of Conflict

If a man faced with a conflict of duties undertakes to deal with them absolutely on his own responsibility, and before a judge who sits in judgment on him day and night, he may well find himself in an isolated position. . . . if only because he is involved in an endless inner trial in which he is his own counsel and ruthless examiner.[20]

Any conflict situation constellates the problem of opposites. Broadly speaking, "the opposites" refers to ego-consciousness and the unconscious. This is true whether the conflict is recognized as an internal one or not, since conflicts with other people are almost always externalizations of an unconscious conflict within oneself. Because they are not made conscious, they are acted out on others through projection.

Whatever the conscious attitude may be, the opposite is in the unconscious. There is no way to haul this out by force. If we try, it will refuse to come. That is why the process of analysis is seldom productive unless there is an active conflict. Indeed, as long as outer life proceeds relatively smoothly, there is no need to deal with the unconscious. But when we are troubled, it is wise to take it into consideration.

The classic conflict situation is one in which there is the possibility of, or temptation to, more than one course of action. Theoretically the options may be many, but in practice a conflict is usually between two, each carrying its own chain of consequences. In such cases the psychological reality is that two separate personalities are involved. It is helpful to think of these as different aspects of oneself; in other words, as personifications of complexes.

---

[20] *Memories, Dreams, Reflections,* p. 345.

Perhaps the most painful conflicts are those involving duty or a choice between security and freedom. Such conflicts generate a great deal of inner tension. As long as they are not conscious, the tension manifests as physical symptoms, particularly in the stomach, the back and the neck. Conscious conflict, on the other hand, is experienced as moral or ethical tension.

I have worked analytically with married men and women who had secret lovers and troubling physical ailments. By and large, they did not come to me because of a conflict over their extramarital activities, which were safely compartmentalized. In truth, they were split and didn't know it. But when their right hand (ego) openly acknowledged what their left hand (shadow) was doing, their physical symptoms disappeared. There then followed moral tension and a conscious search for resolution.

Conflict is a hallmark of neurosis, but conflict is not invariably neurotic. Life naturally involves the collision between conflicting obligations and incompatible desires. Some degree of conflict is even desirable, since without it the flow of life is sluggish. Conflict only becomes neurotic when it settles in and interferes, physically or mentally, with the way one functions.

Two preliminary possibilities exist for resolving a conflict. You can tally up the pro's and con's on each side and reach a logically satisfying decision, or you can opt for what you "really want," then proceed to do what is necessary to make it possible.

Many minor conflicts can be decided by reason. But serious conflicts do not so easily disappear; in fact they often arise precisely because of a one-sided rational attitude, and thus are more likely to be prolonged than solved by reason alone.

Where this is so, it is appropriate to ask, "But what do *I* want?" or alternatively, "What do I *want?*" These are useful questions, for the first, with the accent on "I," clarifies the individual ego position (as opposed to what others might want), and the second, stressing "want," activates the feeling function (judgment, evaluation).

A serious conflict invariably involves a disparity between thinking and feeling. If feeling is not a conscious factor in the conflict, it needs to be introduced; the same may be said for thinking.

If the ego position coincides with, or can accept, the feeling attitude, all well and good. But if these are not compatible and the ego refuses to give way, then the situation remains at an impasse. That is the clinical picture of neurotic conflict, the resolution of which requires a dialogue with one's other sides. We can learn a good deal about ourselves through relationships with others, but the unconscious is a more objective mirror of who we really are.

Jung believed that the potential resolution of a conflict is activated by holding the tension between the opposites. When every motive has an equally strong countermotive—that is, when the conflict between the ego and the unconscious is at its peak—there is a damming up of vital energy. But life cannot tolerate a standstill. If the ego can hold the tension, something quite unexpected emerges, an irrational "third" that effectively resolves the situation.

This irrational "third" is what Jung called the transcendent function, which typically manifests as a symbol. Here is how he described the process:

> [A conflict] requires a real solution and necessitates a third thing in which the opposites can unite. Here the logic of the intellect usually fails, for in a logical antithesis there is no third. The "solvent" can only be of an irrational nature. In nature the resolution of opposites is always an energic process: she acts *symbolically* in the truest sense of the word, doing something that expresses both sides, just as a waterfall visibly mediates between above and below.[21]

Outer circumstances may remain the same, but a change takes place in the individual. This generally appears as a new attitude toward oneself and others; energy previously locked up in a state of indecision is released and once again it becomes possible to move forward.

At that point, it is as if you were to stand on a mountain top watching a raging storm below—the storm may go on, but you are outside of it, to some extent objective, no longer emotionally

---

21 "The Conjunction," *Mysterium Coniunctionis,* CW 14, par. 705.

stressed. There is a sense of peace. This is not essentially different from the traditional Christian concept of grace—"the peace that passeth understanding"—except that it doesn't come from a distant God; it wells up inside.

This process requires patience and an ego strong enough to bend but not break, otherwise a decision will be made out of desperation, just to escape the tension. But when a decision is made prematurely—when the tension has not been held long enough—then the other side, the option that was not chosen, will be constellated even more strongly and we're right back in the fire.

Ah, one asks, but aren't some conflicts intrinsically insoluble?

Well, yes, that may be true in terms of external solutions. But a solution in outer life is as often as not simply avoiding or rationalizing the underlying problem. As Jung writes:

> If a man cannot get on with his wife, he naturally thinks the conflict would be solved if he married someone else. When such marriages are examined they are seen to be no solution at all. The old Adam enters upon the new marriage and bungles it just as badly as he did the earlier one. A real solution comes only from within, and then only because the patient has been brought to a different attitude.[22]

Women are ill-advised to be smug about this passage. Jung, as a product of his time, was not gender-conscious. If he were writing the above today, I dare say he would have reworded it to include women, putting Eve on the hot-seat along with Adam.

---

[22] "Some Crucial Points in Psychoanalysis: A Correspondence between Dr. Jung and Dr. Loÿ," *Freud and Psychoanalysis,* CW 4, par. 606.

9
Man's Inner Woman

The anima is the *archetype of life itself.*[23]

Psychologically a man's inner woman, his anima, functions as his soul. When a man is full of life we say he is "animated." The man with no connection to his feminine side feels dull and listless. Nowadays we call this depression, but the experience is not new. For thousands of years, among so-called primitive peoples, it has been known as loss of soul.

A man's inner image of woman is initially determined by his experience of his personal mother or closest female caregiver. It is later modified through contact with other women—friends, relatives, teachers—but the experience of the personal mother is so powerful and long-lasting that a man is naturally attracted to those women who are much like her—or, as often happens, women quite *unlike* her. That is to say, he may yearn for what he's known, or seek to escape it at all costs.

A man who is unconscious of his feminine side is apt to see that aspect of himself, whatever its characteristics may be, in an actual woman. This happens via projection and is commonly experienced as falling in love or, conversely, as intense dislike. A man may also project his anima onto another man, in love or hate, though in practice this is often difficult to distinguish from the projection of the man's shadow.

A man unrelated to his inner woman tends to be moody, sometimes gentle and sentimental but prone to sudden rage and violence. Analysts call this being anima-possessed. By paying attention to his moods and emotional reactions—objectifying and personifying

[23] "Archetypes of the Collective Unconscious," *The Archetypes and the Collective Unconscious,* CW 9i, par. 66.

them—a man can come into possession of his soul rather than be possessed by it. As with any complex, the negative influence of the anima is reduced by establishing a conscious relationship with it.

Jung distinguished four broad stages of the anima in the course of a man's psychological development. He personified these, in accord with classical stages of eroticism, as Eve, Helen, Mary and Sophia.[24]

In the first stage, Eve, the man's anima is completely tied up with the mother—not necessarily his personal mother, but the archetypal image of woman as faithful provider of nourishment, security and love—or, indeed, the opposite. The man with an anima of this type cannot function well without a vital connection to a woman and is easy prey to being controlled by her. He frequently suffers impotence or has no sexual desire at all.

In the second stage, personified in the historical figure of Helen of Troy, the anima is a collective sexual image. She is Marlene Dietrich, Marilyn Monroe, Tina Turner, Madonna, all rolled up into one. The man under her spell is often a Don Juan who engages in repeated sexual adventures. These will invariably be short-lived, for two reasons: 1) he has a fickle heart—his feelings are whimsical and often gone in the morning—and 2) no real woman can live up to the expectations that go with this unconscious, ideal image.

The third stage of anima development Jung calls Mary. It manifests in religious feelings and a capacity for genuine friendship with women. The man with an anima of this kind is able to see a woman as she is, independent of his own needs. His sexuality is integrated into his life, not an autonomous function that drives him. He can differentiate between love and lust. He is capable of lasting relationships because he can tell the difference between the object of his desire and his inner image of woman.

In the fourth stage, as Sophia (called Wisdom in the Bible), a

---

[24] See "The Psychology of the Transference," *The Practice of Psychotherapy,* CW 16, par. 361; also Marie-Louise von Franz, "The Process of Individuation," in C.G. Jung, *Man and His Symbols,* pp. 185-186.

man's anima functions as a guide to the inner life, mediating to consciousness the contents of the unconscious. Sophia is behind the need to grapple with the grand philosophical issues, the search for meaning. She is Beatrice in Dante's *Inferno,* and the creative muse in any artist's life. She is a natural mate for the archetypal "wise old man" in the male psyche. The sexuality of a man at this stage incorporates a spiritual dimension.

Theoretically, a man's anima development proceeds through these stages as he grows older. When the possibilities of one have been exhausted—which is to say, when adaptation to oneself and outer circumstances requires it—the psyche stimulates the move to the next stage.

In fact, the transition from one stage to another seldom happens without a struggle, for the psyche not only promotes and supports growth, it is also, paradoxically, conservative and loath to give up what it knows. Hence a psychological crisis is commonly precipitated when there is a pressing need for a man to move from one stage to the next.

For that matter, a man may have periodic contact with any number of anima images, at any time of life, depending on what is required to compensate the current dominant conscious attitude. The reality is that psychologically men live in a harem. Any man may observe this for himself by paying close attention to his dreams and fantasies. His soul-image appears in many different forms, as myriad as the expressions of an actual woman's femininity.

In subhuman guise, the anima may manifest as snake, toad, cat or bird; on a slightly higher level, as nixie, pixie, mermaid. In human form—to mention only a few personifications modeled on goddesses in Greek mythology—the anima may appear as Hera, consort and queen; Demeter/Persephone, the mother-daughter team; Aphrodite, the lover; Pallas Athene, carrier of culture and protectress of heroes; Artemis, the stand-offish huntress; and Hecate, ruler in the netherworld of magic.

The assimilation of a particular anima-image results in its death, so to speak. That is to say, as one personification of the anima is consciously understood, it is supplanted by another. Anima development in a man is thus a continuous process of death and rebirth. An understanding of this process is very important in surviving the transition stage between one anima-image and the next. Just as no real woman relishes being discarded for another, so no anima-figure willingly takes second place to her upstart rival. In this regard, as in so much else involved in a person's psychological development, the good is the enemy of the better.[25] To have made contact with your inner woman at all is a blessing; to be tied to one that holds you back can be fatal.

While the old soul-mate clamors for the attention that now, in order for the man to move on, is demanded by and due to the new one, the man is often assailed by conflicting desires. The struggle is not just an inner, metaphorical one; it also involves his lived relationships with real women. The resultant suffering and inner turmoil, the tension and sleepless nights, are comparable to what occurs in any conflict situation.

As the mediating function between the ego and the unconscious, the anima is complementary to the persona and in a compensatory relationship to it. That is to say, all those qualities absent from the outer attitude will be found in the inner. Jung gives the example of a tyrant tormented by bad dreams and gloomy forebodings:

> Outwardly ruthless, harsh, and unapproachable, he jumps inwardly at every shadow, is at the mercy of every mood, as though he were the feeblest and most impressionable of men. Thus his anima contains all those fallible human qualities his persona lacks.[26]

Similarly, when a man identifies with his persona, he is in effect possessed by the anima, with all the attendant symptoms.

> Identity . . . with the persona automatically leads to an unconscious identity with the anima because, when the ego is not differentiated

---

[25] Jung: "If better is to come, good must step aside." ("The Development of Personality," *The Development of Personality,* CW 17, par. 320.

[26] "Definitions," *Psychological Types,* CW 6, par. 804.

> from the persona, it can have no conscious relation to the unconscious processes. Consequently it *is* these processes, it is identical with them. Anyone who is himself his outward role will infallibly succumb to the inner processes; he will either frustrate his outward role by absolute inner necessity or else reduce it to absurdity, by a process of *enantiodromia*.[27] He can no longer keep to his individual way, and his life runs into one deadlock after another. Moreover, the anima is inevitably projected upon a real object, with which he gets into a relation of almost total dependence.[28]

Thus it is essential for a man to distinguish between who he is and who he appears to be. Symptomatically, in fact, there is no significant difference between persona identification and anima possession; both are indications of unconsciousness.

---

[27] Enantiodromia is a term originally coined by the Greek philosopher Heraclitus. Literally it means "running counter to," referring to the emergence of the unconscious opposite in the course of time.

[28] Ibid., par. 807.

10
Woman's Inner Man

A woman possessed by the animus is always in danger of losing her femininity.[29]

A woman's inner man, her animus, is strongly colored by her experience of her personal father. Just as a man is apt to marry his mother, so to speak, so a woman is inclined to favor a man psychologically like her father, or, again, his opposite.

Whereas the anima in a man functions as his soul, a woman's animus is more like an unconscious mind. It manifests negatively in fixed ideas, unconscious assumptions and conventional opinions that may be generally right but just beside the point in a particular situation. A woman unconscious of her masculine side tends to be highly opinionated—animus-possessed. This kind of woman proverbially wears the pants; she rules the roost, or tries to. The men attracted to her will be driven to distraction by her whims, coldly emasculated, while she herself wears a mask of indifference to cover her insecurity. Jung:

> No matter how friendly and obliging a woman's Eros may be, no logic on earth can shake her if she is ridden by the animus. . . . [A man] is unaware that this highly dramatic situation would instantly come to a banal and unexciting end if he were to quit the field and let a second woman carry on the battle (his wife, for instance, if she herself is not the fiery war horse). This sound idea seldom or never occurs to him, because no man can converse with an animus for five minutes without becoming the victim of his own anima.[30]

A woman's animus becomes a helpful psychological factor only when she can tell the difference between her inner man and herself.

---

[29] "Anima and Animus," *Two Essays on Analytical Psychology,* CW 7, par. 337.
[30] "The Syzygy: Anima and Animus," *Aion,* CW 9ii, par. 29.

While a man's task in assimilating the anima involves discovering his true feelings, a woman must constantly question her ideas and opinions, measuring these against what she really thinks. If she does so, in time the animus can become a valuable inner companion who endows her with qualities of enterprise, courage, objectivity and spiritual wisdom.

Jung describes four stages of animus development in a woman, paralleling those of the anima in a man. He first appears in dreams and fantasy as the embodiment of physical power, for instance an athlete or muscle man, a James Bond or Sylvester Stallone. This corresponds to the anima as Eve. For a woman with such an animus a man is simply a stud; he exists to give her physical satisfaction, protection and healthy babies.

In the second stage, analogous to the anima as Helen, the animus possesses initiative and the capacity for planned action. He is behind a woman's desire for independence and a career of her own. However, a woman with an animus of this type still relates to a man on a collective level: he is the generic husband-father, the man around the house whose primary role is to provide shelter and support for his family—Mr. Do-All, Mr. Fix-It, with no life of his own.

In the next stage, corresponding to the anima as Mary, the animus is the Word personified, appearing in dreams as a professor, clergyman, scholar or some other authoritarian figure. A woman with such an animus has a great respect for traditional learning; she is capable of sustained creative work and welcomes the opportunity to exercise her mind. She is able to relate to a man on an individual level, as lover rather than husband or father, and she seriously ponders her own elusive identity.

In the fourth stage, the animus is the incarnation of spiritual meaning—a Mahatma Gandhi, Martin Luther King or Dalai Lama. On this highest level, like the anima as Sophia, the animus mediates between a woman's conscious mind and the unconscious. In mythology he appears as Hermes, messenger of the gods; in dreams he is a helpful guide. Sexuality for such a woman is imbued with spiritual significance.

Any of these aspects of the animus can be projected onto a man, who will be expected to live up to the projected image. As mentioned earlier, the same is true of the anima. So in any relationship between a man and a woman there are at least four personalities involved, as shown in the diagram.[31]

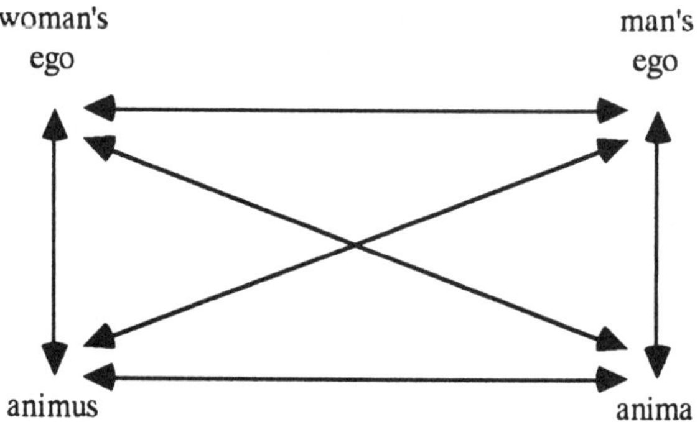

Theoretically, there is no difference between an unconscious man and an unconscious woman's animus. One implication of this is that an unconscious man can be coerced into being or doing whatever a woman wants. But it's just as true the other way around: unconscious women are easily seduced by a man's anima. In relationships there are no innocent victims.

The more differentiated a woman is in her own femininity, the more able she is to reject whatever unsuitable role is projected onto her by a man. This forces the man back on himself. If he has the capacity for self-examination and insight, he may discover in himself the basis for false expectations. Failing inner resources on either side, there is only rancor and animosity.

---

[31] Adapted from Jung's drawing in "The Psychology of the Transference," *The Practice of Psychotherapy,* CW 16, par. 422.

11
True and False Brides/Bridegrooms

The truth of yesterday must be set aside for what is now *the truth of one's psychic life.*[32]

A dominant but inappropriate anima-image in a man's psyche is characterized in fairy tales as a false bride. It is the hero's task to find the true one. The essential difference between the two, psychologically, is captured in the above observation.

True and false brides don't come labeled. Much depends on a man's age, his position in life and how much work he has done on himself—particularly the extent to which he has differentiated his soul-image from the other complexes teeming in his psyche.

Theoretically there are two basic types of false bride. One is an anima figure—or an actual woman—who leads a man into the fantasy realm, away from timely responsibilities in the outside world. The other is an inner voice—or again a real woman—that would tie a man to his persona when his real task is to turn inward, to find himself behind the face he shows others.

The first type is commonly associated with the attitudes of a younger man: idealism, the disinclination to compromise, a rigid response to the reality of everyday life. The second type of false bride is associated with regressive tendencies in later life, such as feverish efforts to mask one's age or reclaim a lost youth through younger companions, face lifts, hair transplants and so on.

There is no hard and fast rule, however. An older man with too much unlived life may have to descend into the whore's cellar, so to speak, as part of his individuation process. The younger man with no ideals may be obliged to develop some.

As happens with any psychological content, the bride of either

[32] Marie-Louise von Franz, *Redemption Motifs in Fairy Tales,* p. 85.

type, when not recognized as an inner reality, appears in the outside world through projection. If a man's anima is lonely and desperate for attention, he will tend to fall in love with dependent women who demand all his time and energy. The man with a mother-bound anima will get tied up with women who want to take care of him. The man not living up to his potential will fall for women who goad him on. In short, whatever qualities a man doesn't recognize in himself—shadow, anima, whatever—will confront him in real life. Outer reflects inner. If there are any psychological rules that are valid always and everywhere, that is one of them.

The seductive lure of the false bride manifests in outer life not only as a tie to an unsuitable woman but also as the wrong choice in a conflict situation. This is due to the regressive tendencies of the unconscious. Each new stage of development, each foothold on an increase in consciousness, must be wrested anew from the dragon-like grip of the past. This process is called by Jung an *opus contra naturam,* a work against nature. That is because nature is essentially conservative and unconscious. There is a lot to be said for the natural mind and the healthy instincts that go with it, but not much in terms of consciousness.

Analogous to these true and false anima-brides, there are true and false bridegrooms. The latter may manifest as a woman's feelings of worthlessness and despair, and in her outer life as a compulsive tie to, say, an authoritarian father figure or an abusive partner. The true bridegroom gives her confidence in herself and encourages her endeavors; as the man in her outer life he is interested in her mind as well as her body.

In the best of all possible worlds, the true bridegroom finds his mate in the true bride, and vice versa. Unfortunately, this is no guarantee that they will live happily ever after. No matter how individuated one is, no matter how much one has worked on oneself, projection and conflict in relationships are always possible, if not inevitable. But that's no bad thing; we are human, after all, and such things prompt us to become more conscious.

12
Relationship Problems in a Nutshell

When animus and anima meet, the animus draws his sword of power and the anima ejects her poison of illusion and seduction. The outcome need not always be negative, since the two are equally likely to fall in love.[33]

We all want someone to love and someone to be loved by. But intimate relationships are fraught with difficulty. There are any number of landmines to be negotiated before two people feel comfortable with each other; more when they become sexually involved, and more again if and when they live together. On top of the twin devils of projection and identification, there are each other's personal complexes and typological differences. In truth, the very things that brought them together in the first place are just as likely to drive them apart.

Most relationships begin with mutual good will. Why, then, do so many end in acrimony? There are probably as many answers to this as there are couples who split up, but in terms of a common pattern, typology certainly plays a major role.

Following the logistics implicit in Jung's model of psychological types,[34] an extraverted man has an introverted anima, while an introverted woman has an extraverted animus, and vice versa. This can change through psychological work on oneself, but these inner images are commonly projected onto persons of the opposite sex, with the result that either attitude type is prone to being fascinated by its opposite. This happens because each type is complementary to the other.

The introvert is inclined to be reflective, to think things out and

---

[33] "The Syzygy: Anima and Animus," *Aion*, CW 9ii, par. 30.
[34] See above, pp. 16f.

consider carefully before acting. Shyness and a degree of distrust result in hesitation and some difficulty in adapting to the external world. The extravert, on the other hand, fascinated by new and unknown situations, tends to act first and think after.

As Jung notes,

> The two types therefore seem created for a symbiosis. The one takes care of reflection and the other sees to the initiative and practical action. When the two types marry they may effect an ideal union.[35]

Discussing such a typical situation, Jung points out that it is ideal only so long as the partners are occupied with their adaptation to "the manifold external needs of life":

> But when . . . external necessity no longer presses, then they have time to occupy themselves with one another. Hitherto they stood back to back and defended themselves against necessity. But now they turn face to face and look for understanding—only to discover that they have never understood one another. Each speaks a different language. Then the conflict between the two types begins. This struggle is envenomed, brutal, full of mutual depreciation, even when conducted quietly and in the greatest intimacy. For the value of the one is the negation of value for the other.[36]

Clearly such a couple has some work to do on their relationship. But that doesn't mean they ought to discuss the psychological meaning or implications of what goes on between them. Far from it. When there is a quarrel or ill feeling in the air, it is quite enough to acknowledge that one is in a bad mood or feels hurt, as opposed to psychologizing the situation with talk of anima/animus, complexes and so on. These are after all only theoretical constructs, and head talk is sure to drive one or the other into a frenzy. Relationships thrive on feeling values, not on what is written in books.

You work on a relationship by shutting your mouth when you are ready to explode; by not inflicting your affect on the other per-

---

[35] *Two Essays on Analytical Psychology,* CW 7, par. 80.
[36] Ibid.

son; by quietly leaving the battlefield and tearing your hair out; by asking yourself—not your partner—what complex in you was activated, and to what end. The proper question is not, "Why is she doing that to me?" or "Who does he think he is?" but rather, "Why am I reacting in this way?—Who do *I* think he or she is?" And more: "What does this say about my psychology? What can I do about it?" Instead of accusing the other person of driving you crazy, you say to yourself, "I feel I'm being driven crazy—where, or who, in me is that coming from?"

That is how you establish a container, a personal *temenos,* a private place where you launder your complexes.

It is true that a strong emotion sometimes needs to be expressed, because it comes not from a complex but from genuine feeling. There is a fine line between the two, and it is extremely difficult to tell one from the other without a container. But when you can tell the difference you can speak from the heart.

Working on a relationship involves keeping your mood to yourself and examining it. You neither bottle up the emotion nor allow it to poison the air. The merit in this approach is that it throws us back entirely on our experience of ourselves. It is foolish to imagine we can change the person who seems to be the cause of our heartache. But with the proper container we can change ourselves and our reactions.

There are those who think that "letting it all hang out" is therapeutic. But that is merely allowing a complex to take over. The trick is to get some distance from the complex, objectify it, take a stand toward it. You can't do this if you identify with it, if you can't tell the difference between yourself and the emotion that grabs you by the throat when a complex is active. And you can't do it without a container.

Those who think that talking about a relationship will help it get better put the cart before the horse. Work on yourself and a good relationship will follow. You can either accept who you are and find a relationship that fits, or twist yourself out of shape and get what you deserve.

The endless blather that takes place between two complexed people solves nothing. It is a waste of time and energy and as often as not actually makes the situation worse.

Of course, as Jung points out in the passage that heads this chapter, the meeting between anima and animus is not always negative. In the beginning the two are just as likely to be starry-eyed lovers. Later, when the bloom is off the rose, they may even become fast friends. But the major battles in close relationships occur because the man has not withdrawn his anima projection on the woman, and/or the woman still projects her animus onto the man.

We may understand this intellectually, but when our loved one does not behave according to the image we have of him or her, we are instantly complexed. Our emotions override what is in our minds. Our reactions run the gamut from violence to anger to grieved silence, and it is bound to happen again, with this one or the next, unless we reflect on what is behind it: our own psychology.

Finally, the reality must be faced that no one relationship can fulfill all our needs, as individuals, all of the time. One partner or other may in time, for reasons of their own, feel drawn to intimacy with another.

Such situations are of course fraught with conflict, both inner and outer, but need not split the two asunder. The feeling function must rule the day: What is my long-standing relationship worth to me? If it is important enough to both, and where love is not wanting, it will survive the turmoil, becoming all the richer for the struggle, and the partners more conscious of who they are.[37]

The pre-requisite for a good marriage, it seems to me,
is the licence to be unfaithful.[38]

---

[37] For more on this theme, see Jung's comments on "the container and the contained" in "Marriage As a Psychological Relationship," *The Development of Personality,* CW 17, pars. 331ff.; also Sharp, *Getting To Know You: The Inside Out of Relationship,* pp. 107ff.

[38] Jung, in William McGuire, ed. *The Freud/Jung Letters,* p. 175.

13
The Self-Regulation of the Psyche

Only what is really oneself has the power to heal.[39]

If I were asked to choose one remark of Jung's that informs my attitude as an analyst, that would be it. The whole process is there, including the idea that neurosis is an attempt at self-cure. And what is really oneself can only be discovered through holding the tension between the opposites until the "third"—something not logically given—manifests. How this third, the so-called transcendent function, makes itself known depends on individual psychology and circumstances. But in Jung's model it always represents the creative intervention and guidance of the Self, the archetype of wholeness, which functions as the regulating center of the psyche.

In plainer words, the Self is a transpersonal power that is beyond the control of the ego. It can be experienced, but not easily defined. In fact, there is no difference between the Self as an experiential, psychological reality and the religious concept of a supreme being, except that the traditional idea of God places Him somewhere "out there." In Jung's model of the psyche, the Self is inside.

Here are some significant comments by Jung on the Self:

> Intellectually the self is no more than a psychological concept, a construct that serves to express an unknowable essence which we cannot grasp as such, since by definition it transcends our powers of comprehension. It might equally well be called the "God within."[40]

> Sensing the self as something irrational, as an indefinable existent, to which the ego is neither opposed nor subjected, but merely at-

[39] *Two Essays on Analytic Psychology*, CW 7, par. 258.

[40] Ibid., par. 399. Note that Jung did not capitalize the word "self," but in modern Jungian writing it is conventional to do so in order to differentiate the Self as archetype from the ego-self.

> tached, and about which it revolves very much as the earth revolves round the sun—thus we come to the goal of individuation.[41]

> So long as the self is unconscious, it corresponds to Freud's super-ego and is a source of perpetual moral conflict. If, however, it is withdrawn from projection and is no longer identical with public opinion, then one is truly one's own yea and nay. The self then functions as a union of opposites and thus constitutes the most immediate experience of the Divine which it is psychologically possible to imagine.[42]

Like any archetype, the essential nature of the Self is unknown and possibly unknowable, but its many and various manifestations—archetypal images—are known to us, in one form or another, as the content of dreams, myth and legend. Jung says it all:

> The self appears in dreams, myths, and fairytales in the figure of the "supraordinate personality," such as a king, hero, prophet, saviour, etc., or in the form of a totality symbol, such as the circle, square, *quadratura circuli,* cross, etc. When it represents a *complexio oppositorum,* a union of opposites, it can also appear as a united duality, in the form, for instance, of *tao* as the interplay of *yang* and *yin,* or of the hostile brothers, or of the hero and his adversary (arch-enemy, dragon), Faust and Mephistopheles, etc. Empirically, therefore, the self appears as a play of light and shadow, although conceived as a totality and unity in which the opposites are united.[43]

Psychologically, uniting the opposites involves first recognizing them in whatever conflict we are engaged in, and then holding the tension between them. The extent to which we are successful in this difficult and often lengthy endeavor—the degree of wholeness we experience—can be called a manifestation of the Self, or, if one prefers, the grace of God.

---

[41] Ibid., par. 405.

[42] "Transformation Symbolism in the Mass," *Psychology and Religion,* CW 11, par. 396.

[43] "Definitions," *Psychological Types,* CW 6, par. 790.

14
Personal Analysis

Analysis should release an experience that grips us or falls upon us from above, an experience that has substance and body such as those things which occurred to the ancients. If I were going to symbolize it I would choose the Annunciation.[44]

You can appreciate the scope of Jung's work, and you can read everything he ever wrote, but the real opportunity offered by analytical psychology only becomes apparent when you go into analysis. That's when Jung's potentially healing message stops being merely an interesting idea and becomes an experiential reality.

Analysis is not a suitable discipline for everyone, nor do all benefit from it or need it. Although there may be as many ways of practicing Jungian analysis as there are analysts, the process itself facilitates healing because it relates what is going on in the unconscious to what is happening in everyday life.

We generally seek a quick fix to our problems. We want an answer, a prescription; we want our pain to be treated, our suffering relieved. We want a solution, and we look for it from an outside authority. This is a legitimate expectation for many physical ills, but it doesn't work with psychological problems, where you are obliged to take personal responsibility for the way things are. Then you have to consider your shadow—and everyone else's—and all the other complexes that drive you and your loved ones up the wall.

What people want and what they need are seldom the same thing. You go into analysis hurting and with some goals and expectations in mind. But pretty soon your personal agenda goes out the window and you find yourself grappling with issues you hadn't thought of and sore spots you didn't know were there—or knew but

[44] Jung, *Seminar 1925*, p. 111.

avoided thinking about. It is very exciting, all this new information about yourself. It's inevitably inflating, and for a while you think you have all the answers—but it can also be quite painful, since things generally get worse before they get better.

It has been said that analysis is only for an elite because it's expensive and time-consuming. It is true that analysis involves a good deal of time and energy and it's not cheap. But I have worked with teachers and taxi-drivers, doctors, actors, politicians, artists—men and women in just about every walk of life—of whom not one was independently wealthy. The fee they paid was no small matter, affordable only by making sacrifices in other areas of their life. It is a matter of priorities—you put your money, your energy, into what you value, and if you hurt enough you find a way.

Jungian analysis is not about improving yourself or making you a better person. It is about becoming conscious of who you are, including your strengths and weaknesses. Analysis is not something that's done to you. It is a joint effort by two people focused on trying to understand what makes you tick.

In the process of working on yourself you will change, and that can create new problems. Others may not like who you become, or you may no longer like them. Indeed, it may be that as many relationships break up through analysis as are cemented. When you become aware of your complexes, and take back what you have projected onto, say, a partner, you may discover there is not much left to hold you together. A difficult experience, but the sooner you realize you aren't in the right place, the better. Analysis makes it possible to live one's experiential truth and accept the consequences.

The particular circumstances that take a person into analysis are as multitudinous as grains of sand on a beach. They are both as unique and as similar as one grain of sand is to another. True, the reasons are always related to one's personal psychology and life situation. But behind such individual details there are general patterns of thought and behavior that have been experienced and expressed since the beginning of mankind. An understanding of these patterns, found the world over in myths, fairy tales and religions—

manifestations of what Jung called the archetypes—gives one a perspective on mundane reality.

A knowledge of archetypes and archetypal patterns is a kind of blueprint, or background, against which our individual complexes are played out. It is an indispensable tool for Jungian analysts, and an overtone that fundamentally distinguishes Jungian analysis from any other form of therapy.

15
The Analytic Process

As long as an analysis moves on the mental plane nothing happens, you can discuss whatever you please, it makes no difference, but when you strike against something below the surface, then a thought comes up in the form of an experience, and stands before you like an object. . . . Whenever you experience a thing that way, you know instantly that it is a fact.[45]

True healing does not happen in the head. It occurs through feeling-toned realizations in response to lived experience. That is why the analytic process, when pursued on an intellectual level—and that includes most self-analysis—is sterile.

Thoughts "in the form of an experience" have a transforming effect because they are numinous, overwhelming. They lead to a more balanced perspective: one is merely human—not entirely good (positive inflation), not entirely bad (negative inflation), but a homogenous amalgam of good and evil. The realization and acceptance of this is a mark of the integrated personality.

The process of assimilating unconscious contents does not happen without work. It requires discipline and concentrated application, and a mind receptive to the numinous.

Jung purposely did not develop a systematic therapeutic method or technique, because he valued what happened in the individual encounter with patients above any theories on how things "should" proceed. He writes:

> No programme can be formulated for the technical application of psychoanalysis. . . . My only working rule is to conduct the analysis as a perfectly ordinary, sensible conversation, and to avoid all appearance of medical magic.

---

[45] *The Visions Seminars,* pp. 337f.

> . . . Any interference on the part of the analyst, with the object of forcing the analysis to follow a systematic course, is a gross mistake . . . . So-called chance is the law and order of psychoanalysis.[46]

And this:

> As far as possible I let pure experience decide the therapeutic aims. . . . The shoe that fits one person pinches another; there is no universal recipe for living. Each of us carries his own life-form within him—an irrational form which no other can outbid.[47]

However, Jung did describe four characteristic stages of the analytic process: *confession, elucidation, education* and *transformation.*[48]

In the first stage, you get things off your chest. Its prototype is the confessional practice of almost all the mystery religions of antiquity and their historical continuation in the Catholic Church. You confess to the analyst everything consciously concealed, repressed, guilt-laden, etc.—thoughts, wishes, fantasies, emotions like fear, hate, aggression and so on, and whatever else about yourself you are not proud of.

In the second stage, elucidation, you become aware of personal unconscious contents that have not been concealed or repressed but rather have never been conscious: dormant character traits, attitudes and abilities. You develop an understanding of complexes, projection, persona and shadow, anima/animus, and become aware of a regulating center in yourself, the so-called Self. This comes about mainly through close attention to your responses to daily events and the nightly images in your dreams.

Once these contents have been assimilated to consciousness, the next task is that of education, which refers to discovering your role

---

[46] "Some Crucial Points in Psychoanalysis," *Freud and Psychoanalysis,* CW 4, pars. 624f.

[47] "Problems of Modern Psychotherapy," *The Practice of Psychotherapy,* CW 16, par. 81.

[48] Ibid., pars. 122ff.; see also Marie-Louise von Franz, *C.G. Jung: His Myth in Our Time,* pp. 66ff.

as a social being—your place in the world, where you fit in according to your talents and abilities. During this stage, it is not uncommon for one's real vocation to become apparent, but surprise!—it may be something you hadn't thought of before.

In the fourth stage, transformation, you become more fully the person you were always meant to be. Unconscious compulsion is replaced by conscious development; aimless activity gives way to a directed focus on what is personally relevant and meaningful. Egocentricity is subsumed by a working relationship with the Self.

This process of maturation, although not the only possible sequence, is essentially what Jung meant by individuation. It takes time and effort and usually involves some sacrifice along the way, but it can happen.

16
The Way of Individuation

Individuation is a process of differentiation, having for its goal the development of the individual personality.[49]

In alchemical writings there is a famous precept known as the Axiom of Maria. It goes like this: "*One becomes two, two becomes three, and out of the third comes the one as the fourth.*"[50] Jung saw this dictum as an apt metaphor for the process of individuation, a progressive advance of consciousness in which conflict plays a profoundly important part.

In brief, *one* stands for the original, paradisiacal state of unconscious wholeness (e.g., childhood); *two* signifies the loss of innocence occasioned by a conflict between opposites (e.g., persona and shadow); *three* points to a potential resolution; *the third* is the transcendent function; and *the one as the fourth* is psychologically equivalent to a transformed state of conscious wholeness.

Thus simply put, individuation is a kind of circular odyssey, a spiral journey, where the aim is to get back to where you started, but knowing where you've been.

The process of individuation, becoming conscious of what is truly unique about oneself, is inextricably tied up with individuality and the development of personality. The first step is to differentiate ourselves from those we have admired and imitated: parents, teachers, mentors of any kind. On top of this, individuality and group identity are incompatible; you can have one or the other, but not both. Jung notes:

> It is really the individual's task to differentiate himself from all oth-

---

[49] "Definitions," *Psychological Types,* CW 6

[50] "Introduction to the Religious and Psychological Problems of Alchemy," *Psychology and Alchemy,* CW 12, par. 26.

> ers and stand on his own feet. All collective identities, such as membership in organizations, support of "isms," and so on, interfere with the fulfillment of this task. Such collective identities are crutches for the lame, shields for the timid, beds for the lazy, nurseries for the irresponsible.[51]

On the other hand, Jung also made it clear that he was not advising people to become antisocial eccentrics. Always he insisted that one must adapt to both inner and outer reality. We cannot individuate in a corner; we need the mirror provided by other people as well as that of the unconscious. Our task, and no easy one at that, is to sort out the reflections.

Marie-Louise von Franz, who worked closely with Jung for over thirty years, when asked to comment on what Jung meant by individuation, said the following:

> Individuation means being yourself, becoming yourself. Nowadays one always uses the cheap word "self-realization," but what one really means is ego-realization. Jung means something quite different. He means the realization of one's own predestined development. That does not always suit the ego, but it is what one intrinsically feels could or should be. We are neurotic when we are not what God meant us to be. Basically, that's what individuation is all about. One lives one's destiny. Then usually one is more humane, less criminal, less destructive to one's environment.[52]

Many years ago, when I had nowhere to go but up, my analyst said to me: "Think of what you've been, what you are now, and what you could be." I still find this a useful reflective exercise in terms of orienting myself on the continuum that is my personal journey of individuation.

---

[51] *Memories, Dreams, Reflections,* p. 342.

[52] "The Geography of the Soul," interview in *In Touch,* Summer 1993, p. 12.

17
Developing a Personality

Personality is the supreme realization of the innate idiosyncrasy of a living being.[53]

Personality develops by slow stages in life. It is the fruit of activity coupled with introspection, and confidence tempered by a healthy dose of self-doubt. On the one hand it is an act of courage flung in the face of life's adversities, the affirmation of who one is and what one believes. On the other hand it involves accepting the immediate conditions of our existence, such as where one finds oneself on this earth and having a physical body.

The twin running mates of personality are individuality and individuation. Individuality refers to the qualities or characteristics that distinguish one person from another. Individuation is a process of differentiation and integration, the aim being to become conscious of one's unique psychological make-up. This is quite different from individualism, which is simply me-first and leads inexorably to alienation from others. The individuating person may be obliged to deviate from collective norms, but all the same retains a healthy respect for them. In Jung's felicitous phrase,

> Individuation does not shut one out from the world, but gathers the world to itself.[54]

What motivates a person to individuate, to develop personality instead of settling for persona? Jung's answer is that it doesn't happen by an act of will, or because others (including Jungian analysts) say it would be useful or advisable:

---

[53] "The Development of Personality," *The Development of Personality,* CW 17, par. 289.

[54] "On the Nature of the Psyche," *The Structure and Dynamics of the Psyche,* CW 8, par. 432.

> Nature has never yet been taken in by well-meaning advice. The only thing that moves nature is causal necessity, and that goes for human nature too. Without necessity nothing budges, the human personality least of all. It is tremendously conservative, not to say torpid. . . . The developing personality obeys no caprice, no command, no insight, only brute necessity; it needs the motivating force of inner or outer fatalities. Any other development would be no better than individualism. . . . [which] is a cheap insult when flung at the natural development of personality.[55]

Simply and naturally, those who know themselves (as opposed to those who say they do) become a magnet for those whose souls long for life. You have to own up to the person you've become. Working on yourself has an inductive effect on others. To my mind this is all to the good, for if enough individuals become more consciously psychologically, then the collective will too, and life on this earth will go on.

The guiding principle is this: Be the one through whom you wish to influence others. Mere talk is hollow. There is no trick, however artful, by which this simple truth can be evaded in the long run. The fact of being convinced, and not the things we are convinced of—that is what has always, and at all times, worked a change in others.

---

[55] "The Development of Personality," *The Development of Personality,* CW 17, par. 293.

18
Togetherness vs. Intimacy with Distance

When a person complains that he is always on bad terms with his wife or the people he loves, and that there are terrible scenes or resistances between them, you will see when you analyze this person that he has an attack of hatred. He has been living in participation mystique *with those he loves. He has spread himself over other people until he has become identical with them, which is a violation of the principle of individuality. Then they have resistances naturally, in order to keep themselves apart.*[56]

One of the greatest single obstacles to a mature relationship is the ideal of togetherness. It is an ideal based on the archetypal motif of wholeness. Find your soul-mate, your other half, and you'll live happily ever after. This is a very old idea. You find it in Greek philosophy, for instance in Plato's *Symposium,* where Aristophanes pictures humans as originally whole but arrogant.[57] As punishment, Zeus cut them in half, and now, it is said, we forever seek to replace our lost other.

There is nothing intrinsically wrong with this ideal. The mistake is in expecting to find our "lost other" in the outside world. In fact, it is our contrasexual inner other, animus or anima, who is more properly the object of our search. Outer relationships, already hampered by personal complexes and a multitude of day-to-day concerns, cannot bear the extra weight of archetypal expectations. Although individuation is not possible without relationship, it is not compatible with togetherness.

After the passage quoted above, Jung continues:

---

[56] *The Psychology of Kundalini Yoga: Notes of the Seminar Given in 1932 by C.G. Jung,* p. 7.
[57] *Symposium,* 14-16 (189A-193E).

> I say, "Of course it is most regrettable that you always get into trouble, but don't you see what you are doing? You love somebody, you identify with them, and of course you prevail against the objects of your love and repress them by your very self-evident identity. You handle them as if they were yourself, and naturally there will be resistances. It is a violation of the individuality of those people, and it is a sin against your own individuality. Those resistances are a most useful and important instinct: you have resistances, scenes, and disappointments so that you may become finally conscious of yourself, and then hatred is no more."[58]

Individuation, finding your own unique path, requires a focus on the inner axis, ego to unconscious—getting to know yourself. The ideal of togetherness lets you off that hook. Togetherness doesn't acknowledge the natural boundaries between people, and it gives short shrift to their differences. All you're left with is unconscious identity. When you are on the path of individuation, focused on your own psychological development, you relate to others from a position of personal integrity. This is the basis for intimacy with distance. It is not as sentimental as togetherness, but it's not as sticky either.

A relationship based on intimacy with distance does not require separate living quarters. Intimacy with distance means psychological separation, which comes about through the process of differentiation—knowing where you end and the other begins. Intimacy with distance can be as close and as warm as you want, and it's psychologically clean. Togetherness is simply fusion, the submersion of two individualities into one, variously called symbiosis, identification, *participation mystique*. It can feel good for a while but in the long run it does not work.

Togetherness is to intimacy with distance as being in love is to loving. When you're in love, you absolutely need the other. This is symptomatic of bonding, which is natural between parent and infant, and also at the beginning of any relationship at any age. But

---

[58] *The Psychology of Kundalini Yoga,* p. 7.

need, finally, is not compatible with loving; it only shows the degree to which one lacks personal resources. Better take your need to a therapist than dump it on the one you love. Need in an intimate relationship easily becomes the rationale for power, leading to the fear of loss on one hand, and resentment on the other.

The key to intimacy with distance is the self-containment of each of the partners, which in turn depends on how much they know about themselves. When you are self-contained, psychologically independent, you don't look to another person for completion. You don't identify with others and you're not victimized by their projections. You know where you stand and you live by your personal truth—come what may. You can survive cold shoulders and you can take the heat.

When you are self-contained, you have your own sacred space, your own *temenos.* You might invite someone in, but you're not driven to, and you don't feel abandoned if the invitation is declined. You respect the loved ones' boundaries, their freedom and privacy, even their secrets; you give them space and you don't knowingly push their buttons. You don't judge and you don't blame. There is interest in, and empathy for, the concerns of others, but you don't take them on as your own.

When you are psychologically separate, not identified with your mate, you don't need the other to agree with you and you don't need to be right. You don't expect the other to change in order to suit your needs, and you don't ask it of yourself either. And if over time you can't accept the other but still can't leave, well, that is the stuff of analysis: conflict and complexes.

The bond between two people is a precious and mysterious thing, not entirely explained by the theory of complexes and the phenomenon of projection. But this much at least is true: there is an optimum distance in every relationship that evolves through trial and error and good will—if you know who you are and can stop pressing for more than you get.

19
The Heroic Journey

He is no hero who never met the dragon, or who, if he once saw it, declared afterwards that he saw nothing. Equally, only one who has risked the fight with the dragon and is not overcome by it wins the hoard, the "treasure hard to attain."[59]

Traditionally, in folklore and myth, it is a hero's task to do something out of the ordinary. Overcoming dragons certainly fits the bill. But when you think about it metaphorically, we are all potentially heroes, for we all have our inner demons, a.k.a. dragons.

On a personal, everyday level, meeting the dragon corresponds to becoming aware that our emotional reactions are determined by unconscious factors, namely complexes with a will of their own. Fighting the dragon involves coming to terms with these complexes, part and parcel of which is the ongoing effort to understand why we act or react the way we do.

For those who have a mind for this way of seeing things, dreams, and often outer life too, take on the flavor of a myth or a fairy tale. There are wicked witches (negative mother) and fairy godmothers (positive mother); wizards and elves, demons and wise old men (aspects of the father); helpful animals (instincts) to guide one through the forest (daily life). There are crystal balls (intuition) and rolling skeins of thread (markers on the way); magic hats and cloaks (attitudes); thorns and needles that prick (projections); fearsome giants (complexes) that knock you off your feet (personal standpoint); princesses (eros, feminine energy) held captive in towers (logos ideals), and handsome princes (positive masculine energy) scaling mountains (self-knowledge) to rescue them.

As a matter of fact, I have seldom come across a motif in a

---

[59] *Mysterium Coniunctionis,* CW 14, par. 756.

dream that could not also be found in a myth, legend or fairy tale. This is one of the best-kept secrets of psychological development: others have been through the same tortuous trials. And many have survived.

A sword-fight in a dream may reflect the cut-and-thrust of an encounter with your boss, your lover, your mother; the thorn hedge surrounding a sleeping beauty is a prickly animus who keeps you at bay; the ravishing pixie who lures you to bed may be a false bride, a *femme fatale;* the secretary guarding the photocopier is a witch in high heels; an outworn conscious attitude is a sickly old king; an absent queen reflects lack of feeling; a quarrelsome royal couple is a conflict between masculine and feminine, ego and anima/animus, you and your mate; nightmares of burglars breaking in suggest shadow sides of oneself demanding recognition; and on and on.

Like the Dummling or youngest brother in many fairy tales, it is appropriate to be naive about the unconscious and what it holds. This actually works in one's favor, since accomplishing some of the tasks required of us is only possible if we suspend a rational way of looking at things. The Dummling represents an aspect of the individual psyche that has not been coerced by collective pressures. We all had it at first, and still do, buried under the accretions of daily life: a virgin innocence unhobbled by hard knocks; fresh, spontaneous and not yet fixed in rigid patterns; a time when the border between fantasy and reality was permeable. That openness to the unknown is an important element in the struggle to discover our own individual truth.

The treasure "hard to attain" is variously symbolized in myth and fairy tale as a ring or golden egg, white feather, coat of many colors, fountain of youth, elixir of life, and so on. Psychologically these all come to the same thing: *oneself*—the acceptance of one's true feelings and talents, one's uniqueness. This pursuit, by many other names, is a time-honored tradition. It differs greatly in detail, but the pattern is well known.

Symbolically, the heroic journey is a round, as illustrated in the diagram below.[60] Among other things, it involves a dangerous trial of some kind, psychologically analogous, writes Jung, to "the attempt to free ego-consciousness from the deadly grip of the unconscious."[61] It is a motif represented by imprisonment, crucifixion, dismemberment, abduction—the kind of experience weathered by sun-gods and other heroes since time immemorial: Gilgamesh, Osiris, Christ, Dante, Odysseus, Aeneas, Pinocchio, and Dorothy in *The Wizard of Oz*. In the language of the mystics it is called the dark night of the soul. In everyday life, we know it as a feeling of deep despair and a desire to hide under the covers.

Typically, in myth and legend, the hero journeys by ship or braves dark forests, burning deserts, ice fields, etc. He fights a sea monster or dragon, is swallowed, struggles against being bitten or crushed to death, and having arrived inside the belly of the whale, like Jonah, seeks the vital organ and cuts it off, thereby winning

---

60 Adapted from Joseph Campbell, *The Hero with a Thousand Faces*, p. 245.
61 *Symbols of Transformation*, CW 5, par. 539.

release. Eventually the hero must return to his beginnings and bear witness, that is, give something back to his culture (which marks the hero as an individual as opposed to an individualist).

The night sea journey myths are an important subset of these hero tales. They derive from the perceived behavior of the sun, which, in Jung's lyrical image, "sails over the sea like an immortal god who every evening is immersed in the maternal waters and is born anew in the morning."[62] The sun going down, analogous to the loss of energy in a depression, is thus the necessary prelude to rebirth. Cleansed in the healing waters, the ego lives again. Or, in another mythological image, it rises from the ashes, like the phoenix.

Psychologically, the whale-dragon-monster is the unconscious, and in particular the parental complexes. The battles and suffering that take place during the night sea journey symbolize the heroic attempt to assimilate unconscious contents instead of being overwhelmed by them. Symbolically, the vital organ that must be severed is the umbilical cord, the regressive tie to the past. The potential result is the release of energy—the sun on a new day—that has hitherto been tied up with the complexes.

Few choose the hero's journey. But when something in us demands it we are obliged to strike out on our own, to live out our personal journey whether we will or no.

Analysts cannot save people from the hazards to be faced, nor should they even try. What nature has ordained, let no one interfere with. The heroic journey is an inner imperative that must be allowed to run its course. The most analysts can do is to accompany their charges and alert them to some dangers along the way.

Because individuality and the development of personality are deviations not congenial to the collective, historically only a few have dared the adventure, but these are the ones we now invoke to give us heart. As Jung notes:

> [They] are as a rule the legendary heroes of mankind, the very ones who are looked up to, loved, and worshipped, the true sons of God

[62] Ibid., par. 306.

> whose names perish not. . . . Their greatness has never lain in their abject submission *to* convention, but, on the contrary, in their deliverance *from* convention. They towered up like mountain peaks above the mass that still clung to its collective fears, its beliefs, laws, and systems, and boldly chose their own way.[63]

From the beginning of recorded time, heroes have been endowed with godlike attributes. Historically, anyone who turned aside from the beaten path was deemed to be either crazy or possessed by a demon, or possibly a god. Some were coddled, just in case; the unlucky ones were hacked to pieces or burned at the stake.

Now we have depth psychology. On a collective level we still have heroes—athletes, actors, politicians and the like—and some of these we treat like gods. But we no longer expect of them anything as elusive and differentiated as personality. Individually, however, we have raised our sights. Thanks to Jung we now know that personality, in any substantial use of the term, depends upon a harmonious mix of ego, persona and shadow, in helpful alliance with anima or animus, our contrasexual other, *plus* a working relationship with something greater, like the Self.

Call it God or the Self, or by any other name, without contact with an inner center we have to depend on will power, which is not enough to save us from ourselves, nor to forge a personality out of a sow's ear.

---

[63] "The Development of Personality," *The Development of Personality,* CW 17, par. 298.

20
Dream On

Dreams are neither deliberate nor arbitrary fabrications; they are natural phenomena which are nothing other than what they pretend to be. They do not deceive, they do not lie, they do not distort or disguise. . . . They are invariably seeking to express something that the ego does not know and does not understand.[64]

I never had any dreams before I went into analysis. At least I never remembered them. Well, that's not quite true. When I was six I fell asleep on the toilet and dreamed God came and told me everything would be fine. And I vaguely recall other childhood dreams of magical gardens peopled with elves and fairies.

According to research into the physiology of sleep, we all dream several times a night, shown by so-called REM phenomena—rapid eye movements. People deprived of the level of sleep at which dreams occur soon become anxious and irritable. These experiments, while silent about the content or meaning of dreams, suggest they have an important biological function. But Jung went further: he believed that the purpose of dreams was to monitor and regulate the flow of energy in the psyche.

As an adult, then, I must have had dreams, but for lack of attention they died in the water. Why would I be interested in dreams anyway? I was a child of the Enlightenment. Science, reason and logic were the credos I lived by. Dreams happen at night and have nothing to do with me. That's what I thought until I woke up one morning with a dream that shook me to the core. Here it is:

> I am on a street in the center of a deserted city, surrounded by cavernous buildings. I am chasing a ball that keeps bouncing between

---

[64] "Analytical Psychology and Education," ibid., par. 189.

> the buildings, from one side to the other. It keeps getting away from me; I cannot not pin it down.

I woke up in a cold sweat, terrified, sobbing uncontrollably. From this distance it seems quite innocuous. At the time it blew my world apart. And I have seldom had a dreamless night since.

It was my introduction to the reality of the psyche—a baptism by fire. I did not know that something could be going on in me without my being aware of it. I believed that will power could accomplish anything. "Where there's a will there's a way." My bouncing ball dream came in the midst of a mighty conflict which I had a will to solve but no way. I kept thinking I could deal with it by myself. My reaction to the dream killed that illusion.

Jung describes dreams as independent, spontaneous manifestations of the unconscious, self-portraits, symbolic statements of what is going on in the psyche. Although they are not more important than what goes on during the day, they are helpful comments from the unconscious on our outer life.

Freud's view was that dreams have a wish-fulfilling and sleep-preserving function. Jung acknowledged this to be true in some cases but focused on the role dreams play in the self-regulation of the psyche. He suggested that their main function was to compensate conscious attitudes—to call attention to different points of view—in order to produce an adjustment in the ego-personality.

Compensation is a process aimed at establishing or maintaining balance in the psyche. If the conscious attitude is too one-sided, the dream takes the opposite tack; if the conscious attitude is more or less appropriate, the dream seems satisfied with pointing out minor variations; and if the conscious attitude is entirely adequate, then the dream may even coincide with and support it.

Jung also emphasized the prospective function of dreams, which means that in many cases their symbolic content outlines the solution of a conscious conflict. This is in line with his view of neurosis as purposeful: the aim of dreams is to present to consciousness the information needed to restore the psyche to a healthy balance.

It takes hard work to understand dreams because we aren't used to their symbolic language. Dream images are linked together in a way that is often quite foreign to a linear way of thinking. One of my own more memorable dreams was of a spider on skis, balanced on a razor blade, racing down an Alpine slope. Apparently the unconscious has a sense of humor.

According to Jung, a dream is an interior drama:

> The whole dream-work is essentially subjective, and a dream is a theatre in which the dreamer is himself the scene, the player, the prompter, the producer, the author, the public, and the critic.[65]

In other words, the dream *is* the dreamer. Each element in a dream refers to an aspect of the dreamer's own personality, which means that the people in our dreams are personifications of our complexes. More: dreams show our complexes at work in determining our attitudes, which are in turn responsible for much of our behavior.

Doing the work required to understand the message of a particular dream or dream series is one way to depotentiate complexes, because through this focused attention we establish a conscious relationship to them. However, our own dreams are particularly difficult to understand because our blind spots—our complexes—always get in the way to some extent. Even Jung, after working on thousands of his own dreams over a period of fifty years, confessed to this frustration.

Contrary to popular belief, it is virtually impossible to interpret a dream without the dreamer's cooperation. You need a thorough knowledge of both the context—the dreamer's real-life situation at the time of the dream—and the dreamer's conscious attitude. These, and personal associations to the images in the dream, can only come from the dreamer. If the essential purpose of a dream is to compensate conscious attitudes, you have to know what these are or the dream will forever remain a mystery.

---

[65] "General Aspects of Dream Psychology," *The Practice of Psychotherapy,* CW 16, par. 509.

The exception to this is archetypal dreams. These are distinguished by their impersonal nature and the presence of symbolic images and motifs common to myths and religions all over the world. They commonly appear at times of emotional crisis, when one is experiencing a situation that involves a more or less universal human problem. They also tend to occur at times when a new adjustment or change in the conscious attitude is imperative, and particularly at periods of transition from one stage of life to another, such as puberty, marriage and midlife.

In this category are dreams of natural disasters: earthquakes, hurricanes and other catastrophic, end-of the world images. Only the psychologically naive take these to the streets proclaiming an impending apocalypse. The rest of us look to ourselves. What earth-shattering change is afoot in me? What is rocking my life? What is there about my attitude that the unconscious is unhappy with?

There is no fixed meaning to symbols or motifs in dreams, no valid interpretation that is independent of the psychology and life situation of the dreamer. Thus routine recipes and definitions such as those found in traditional "dream dictionaries" are of no value whatever. Nor are exercises aimed at controlling or manipulating the content of dreams, as some claim to do. There is no convincing evidence that this is possible, nor would it be desirable even if it were, for one would thereby lose valuable information about oneself that is not available otherwise.

Many dreams have a classic dramatic structure. There is an *exposition* (place, time and characters), which shows the initial situation of the dreamer. In the second phase there is *action,* a development in the plot. The third phase is the culmination or *climax*—a decisive event. The final phase is the *lysis,* the result or solution of the action in the dream. It is often helpful to look at the lysis as showing where the dreamer's energy wants to go. Where there is no lysis, no solution is in sight.

The best way to work on one's dreams is in a dialogue with another person, preferably someone trained to look at dreams objectively and therefore less likely to project his or her own psychology onto their images. Of course, even some knowledge of one's own complexes is no guarantee against projection, but without training of some kind both parties are whistling in the dark.

The first step in working with dreams is to get the dreamer's personal associations to all the images in it. If there is a tree, say, or a rug or a snake or apple, it is important to determine what these mean in the experience of the dreamer. This takes the form of circumambulating the image, which means staying close to it: "What does an elephant mean to you?" . . . "What else?" . . . "And what else?" This is quite different from the traditional Freudian method of free association, which may eventually get to the complex but misses the significance of the image.

On top of personal associations to dream images there are often relevant amplifications—what trees or rugs or snakes or apples have meant to other people in other cultures at other times. A knowledge of archetypal images and motifs serves to broaden conscious awareness by bringing in material that is not personally known but is present in the unconscious as part of everyone's psychic heritage.

Garnering personal and archetypal associations to a dream, and its context in the dreamer's waking life, is a relatively simple procedure. It is necessary, but only preparation for the real work—the actual interpretation of the dream and what it is saying about the dreamer's conscious attitudes. This is an exacting task and an experience so intimate that the interpretation of any particular dream is really only valid for the two persons working on it.

In general, dreams may be interpreted on a subjective or an objective level, and sometimes both are relevant. The former approach considers a dream strictly in terms of the dreamer's own psychology. If a person I know appears in my dream, the focus is not on that actual person but on him or her as an image or symbol of projected unconscious contents. Where I have a vital connection with that person, however, an objective interpretation may be more to the point; the dream may be commenting on a significant aspect of our relationship.

In either case, the image of the other person derives from my own psychology. But whether a subjective or objective approach is more valid, or some balance in between, has to be determined from the context of the dream and the personal associations. That is the work of analysis.

Dreams invariably have more than one meaning. Ten analysts can look at a dream and come up with ten different interpretations, depending on their typology and their own complexes. That is why there is no valid interpretation without dialogue, and why the dreamer must have the final say. What "clicks" for the dreamer is "right"—but only for the moment, because subsequent events and later dreams often throw new light on previous interpretations.

21
The Upside of Neurosis

Neurosis is really an attempt at self-cure. . . . It is an attempt of the self-regulating psychic system to restore the balance, in no way different from the function of dreams—only rather more forceful and drastic.[66]

What is meant by the term "neurosis"? What marks a person as "neurotic"? The American Heritage Dictionary gives this definition of neurosis:

> Any of various functional disorders of the mind or emotions, without obvious lesion or change, and involving anxiety, phobia, or other abnormal behavior symptoms.

More simply put, neurosis is a pronounced state of disunity with oneself. We have all, at one time or another, experienced this.

Jung's view was that an acute outbreak of neurosis is purposeful, an opportunity to become conscious of who we are as opposed to who we think we are. By working through the symptoms that regularly accompany neurosis—anxiety, fear, depression, guilt and particularly conflict—we become aware of our limitations and discover our true strengths.

In any breakdown in conscious functioning, energy regresses and unconscious contents are activated in an attempt to compensate the one-sidedness of consciousness.

> Neuroses, like all illnesses, are symptoms of maladjustment. Because of some obstacle—a constitutional weakness or defect, wrong education, bad experiences, an unsuitable attitude, etc.—one shrinks from the difficulties which life brings and thus finds oneself back in the world of the infant. The unconscious compensates this regres-

[66] "The Tavistock Lectures," *The Symbolic Life*, CW 18, par. 389.

> sion by producing symbols which, when understood objectively, that is, by means of comparative research, reactivate general ideas that underlie all such natural systems of thought. In this way a change of attitude is brought about which bridges the dissociation between man as he is and man as he ought to be.[67]

Jung called his attitude toward neurosis energic or final, since it was based on the potential progression of energy rather than the Freudian view that looked for causal or mechanistic reasons for its regression. The two views are not incompatible but rather complementary: the mechanistic approach looks to the personal past for the cause of psychic discomfort in the present; Jung focused on difficulties in the present with an eye to future possibilities. Thus, instead of delving deeply into how and why one arrived at an impasse, he asked: "What is the necessary task which the patient will not accomplish?"[68]

Jung did not dispute Freudian theory that Oedipal fixations can manifest as neurosis in later life. He also acknowledged that certain periods in life, and particularly infancy, often have a permanent and determining influence on the personality. But he found this to be an insufficient explanation for those cases in which there was no trace of neurosis until the time of the breakdown.

> Freud's sexual theory of neurosis is grounded on a true and factual principle. But it makes the mistake of being one-sided and exclusive; also it commits the imprudence of trying to lay hold of unconfinable Eros with the crude terminology of sex. In this respect Freud is a typical representative of the materialistic epoch, whose hope it was to solve the world riddle in a test-tube.[69]

> The psychological determination of a neurosis is only partly due to an early infantile predisposition; it must be due to some cause in the present as well. And if we carefully examine the kind of infantile fantasies and occurrences to which the neurotic is attached, we shall

---

[67] "The Philosophical Tree," *Alchemical Studies,* CW 13, par. 473.
[68] "Psychoanalysis and Neurosis," *Freud and Psychoanalysis,* CW 4, par. 570.
[69] "The Eros Theory," *Two Essays on Analytical Psychology,* CW 7, par. 33.

> be obliged to agree that there is nothing in them that is specifically neurotic. Normal individuals have pretty much the same inner and outer experiences, and may be attached to them to an astonishing degree without developing a neurosis.[70]

What then determines why one person becomes neurotic while another, in similar circumstances, does not? Jung's answer is that the individual psyche knows both its limits and its potential. If the former are being exceeded, or the latter not realized, a breakdown occurs. The psyche itself acts to correct the situation.

> There are vast masses of the population who, despite their notorious unconsciousness, never get anywhere near a neurosis. The few who are smitten by such a fate are really persons of the "higher" type who, for one reason or another, have remained too long on a primitive level. Their nature does not in the long run tolerate persistence in what is for them an unnatural torpor. As a result of their narrow conscious outlook and their cramped existence they save energy; bit by bit it accumulates in the unconscious and finally explodes in the form of a more or less acute neurosis.[71]

Jung's view of neurosis differs radically from the classical psychoanalytic reductive approach, but it does not substantially change what happens in analysis. Activated fantasies still have to be brought to light, because the energy needed for life is attached to them. The object, however, is not to reveal a supposed root cause of the neurosis—its origin in infancy or early life—but to establish a connection between consciousness and the unconscious that will result in the renewed progression of energy.

The operative question in such situations is just this: "Where does my energy want to go?" The answer—not so easy to come by, and even more difficult to act upon—points the way to psychological health.

---

[70] "Psychoanalysis and Neurosis," *Freud and Psychoanalysis,* CW 4, par. 564.

[71] "The Function of the Unconscious," *Two Essays on Analytical Psychology,* CW 7, par. 291.

22
On Becoming Conscious

The reason why consciousness exists, and why there is an urge to widen and deepen it, is very simple: without consciousness things go less well.[72]

One of Jung's basic beliefs, and arguably his most important message, is that the purpose of human life is to become conscious. "As far as we can discern," he writes, "the sole purpose of human existence is to kindle a light in the darkness of mere being."[73] Part and parcel of this is achieving a balance, a right harmony, between mind and body, spirit and instinct. When we go too far one way or the other we become neurotic. Jung says it in one pithy sentence:

> Too much of the animal distorts the civilized man, too much civilization makes sick animals.[74]

The "civilized man" tends to live in his head. He prides himself on a rational approach to life, and rightly so. We are no longer apes. Thanks to reason, science and logic, instead of hanging from trees or living in them, we cut them down to build houses, which we then fill with appliances in order to make life easier, or, as it happens, more complicated.

All the same, the more we lose touch with our other side, our instinctual base, the more likely it is that something will happen in us to bring about a proper balance. This is the basis for Jung's idea of compensation within the psyche. One way or another, we'll be brought down to earth. It is just when we think we have everything under control that we are most apt to fall on our face, and this is

---

[72] "Analytical Psychology and 'Weltanschauung,' " *The Structure and Dynamics of the Psyche,* CW 8, par. 695.

[73] *Memories, Dreams, Reflections,* p. 326.

[74] "The Eros Theory," *Two Essays on Analytical Psychology,* CW 7, par. 32.

especially true when we don't reckon with the uncivilized, ten-million-year-old animal in us.

That being said, unexamined instinctual behavior is a hallmark of unconsciousness and a notable characteristic of the undeveloped personality. Through analysis one can become conscious of the instincts and the many ways in which we are slaves to them. But this is not done with a view to giving them boundless freedom. The aim is rather to incorporate them into a purposeful whole.

Jung defined consciousness as "the function or activity which maintains the relation of psychic contents to the ego."[75] In that way he distinguished it conceptually from the psyche itself, which is comprised of both consciousness *and* the unconscious. Also, although we speak of ego-consciousness, in Jung's model the ego is not the same thing as consciousness, but simply the dominant complex of the conscious mind. Of course, in practice we can only become aware of psychic contents by means of the ego. In other words, the more we know about what's going on in our unconscious, the more conscious we become.

Becoming conscious preeminently involves discriminating between opposites. Since the basic opposites are consciousness and the unconscious, the first hurdle is to acknowledge that there are some things about ourselves we're not aware of. Those who cannot do this are doomed forever to skim the surface of life. For those who can admit to another side of themselves, there is then the daunting task of discriminating between a whole range of other opposites—thinking and feeling, masculine and feminine, good and evil, and so on. And then there is the crucial difference between inner and outer, oneself and others.

Jung describes two distinct ways in which consciousness is enlarged. One is during a moment of high emotional tension involving a situation in the outer world. We feel uneasy for no obvious reason, or strangely attracted to someone, and suddenly we understand what's going on. The other way is what happens in a state of quiet

---

[75] "Definitions," *Psychological Types,* CW 6, par. 700.

contemplation, where ideas pass before the mind's eye like dream-images. Suddenly there is a flash of association between two apparently disconnected and widely separated thoughts. In each case it is the discharge of energy-tension that produces consciousness. These sudden realizations and flashes of insight are what we commonly experience as revelations.

In Jung's model of the psyche, consciousness is a kind of superstructure based on the unconscious and arising out of it:

> Consciousness does not create itself—it wells up from unknown depths. In childhood it awakens gradually, and all through life it wakes each morning out of the depths of sleep from an unconscious condition. It is like a child that is born daily out of the primordial womb of the unconscious. . . . It is not only influenced by the unconscious but continually emerges out of it in the form of spontaneous ideas and sudden flashes of thought.[76]

Elsewhere he uses a different metaphor:

> In the child, consciousness rises out of the depths of unconscious psychic life, at first like separate islands, which gradually unite to form a "continent," a continuous land-mass of consciousness. Progressive mental development means, in effect, extension of consciousness.[77]

A child lives in a state of oneness with its primary care-giver. There is little separation between subject and object. As the growing child assimilates experience and develops personal boundaries—a sense of self separate from the outside world—so the ego comes into being. There is a recognizable sense of personal identity, an "I am." This goes on in fits and starts, until at some point you have this metaphorical "land-mass of consciousness," surrounded by the waters of the unconscious.

The first half of life generally involves this developmental proc-

---

[76] "The Psychology of Eastern Meditation," *Psychology and Religion,* CW 11, par. 935.

[77] "The Development of Personality," *The Development of Personality,* CW 17, par. 326.

ess. Given decent mirroring in the early years, we stand a good chance of acquiring a healthy ego. But again, this is not the same thing as being conscious. There are lots of take-charge people with very healthy egos—captains of industry, politicians, artists, entrepreneurs and so on—who are quite unconscious. You can be a leader, run things like a clock and manage others well. But if you don't take the time to introspect, to question who you are without your external trappings, you can't claim to be conscious.

Mature consciousness, according to Jung, is dependent on a working relationship between a strong but flexible ego and the Self, regulating center of the psyche. For that to happen one has to acknowledge that the ego is not in charge. This is not a natural process; it is a major shift in perspective, like the difference between thinking the earth is the center of the solar system and then learning that the sun is. This generally doesn't happen until later in life, when you look back on your experience and realize there was more going on than you knew. Ergo, something other than "you" was pulling the strings.

Becoming conscious, then, is above all not a one-time thing. It is a continuous process, *by* the ego, of assimilating what was previously unknown *to* the ego. It involves a progressive understanding of why we do what we do. And a major step is to become aware of the many ways we're influenced by unconscious aspects of ourselves, which is to say, our complexes.

Jung visualized the unconscious as an ocean, because both are inexhaustible. Freud saw the unconscious, or subconscious, as little more than a garbage can of fantasies and emotions that were active when we were children and then were repressed or forgotten. Jung accepted that for a while. He was an early champion of Freud's dogma, but in the end it just didn't accord with Jung's own experience. Jung came to believe instead that the unconscious also includes contents we never knew were there: things about ourselves in our personal unconscious, and then, at a deeper level, the collective unconscious, all the varied experiences of the human race, the stuff of myth and religion—a vast historical warehouse. Under the right circumstances, any of this, at any time, can become conscious. Jung writes:

> Everything of which I know, but of which I am not at the moment thinking; everything of which I was once conscious but have now forgotten; everything perceived by my senses, but not noted by my conscious mind; everything which, involuntarily and without paying attention to it, I feel, think, remember, want, and do; all the future things that are taking shape in me and will sometime come to consciousness: all this is the content of the unconscious.[78]

And that is why, in spite of our best efforts, we will all, always, be more or less unconscious.

---

[78] "On the Nature of the Psyche," *The Structure and Dynamics of the Psyche,* CW 8, par. 382.

23
Self-Knowledge and Statistics

The psychological rule says that
when an inner situation is not made conscious,
it happens outside, as fate.[79]

People generally confuse self-knowledge with knowledge of their ego-personalities. Indeed, those with any awareness at all take it for granted that they know themselves. But the real psychic facts are for the most part hidden, since the ego knows only its own contents. Without some knowledge of the unconscious and its contents one cannot claim to know oneself.

Self-knowledge is a matter of getting to know your own individual facts. Theories, notes Jung, are of little help:

> The more a theory lays claim to universal validity, the less capable it is of doing justice to the individual facts. Any theory based on experimentation is necessarily *statistical;* it formulates an *ideal average* which abolishes all exceptions at either end of the scale and replaces them by an abstract mean. This mean is quite valid, though it need not necessarily occur in reality. . . . The exceptions at either end, though equally factual, do not appear in the final result at all, since they cancel each other out.[80]

Jung gives this example:

> If, for instance, I determine the weight of each stone in a pile of pebbles and get an average weight of five ounces, this tells me very little about the real nature of the pebbles. Anyone who thought, on the basis of these findings, that he could pick up a pebble of five ounces at the first try would be in for a serious disappointment. Indeed, it might well happen that however long he searched he would not find a single pebble weighing exactly five ounces.

[79] "Christ, A Symbol of the Self," *Aion,* CW 9ii, par. 126.
[80] "The Undiscovered Self," *Civilization in Transition,* CW 10, par. 493.

> . . . The distinctive thing about real facts, however, is their individuality. Not to put too fine a point on it, one could say that the real picture consists of nothing but exceptions to the rule . . . .
>
> These considerations must be borne in mind whenever there is talk of a theory serving as a guide to self-knowledge. There is and can be no self-knowledge based on theoretical assumptions, for the object of this knowledge is . . . a relative exception and an irregular phenomenon.[81]

Similarly, in the treatment of psychic suffering, Jung stressed that the scientific knowledge of humankind in general must take second place; the important thing is the particular person. On the one hand the analyst is equipped with statistical truths, and on the other is faced with someone who requires individual understanding. One need not deny the validity of statistics, but the more schematic the treatment, the more resistances it calls up in the patient. The analyst therefore needs to have a kind of two-way thinking: doing one thing while not losing sight of the other.

The recognition that there is an unconscious side of ourselves has fundamentally altered the pursuit of self-knowledge. It is apparent now that we are twofold beings: we have a conscious side we more or less know, and an unconscious side of which we know little but which is generally no secret to others. When we lack knowledge of our other side, we can do the most terrible things without calling ourselves to account and without ever suspecting what we're doing. Thus we may be baffled by how others react to us. The increased self-knowledge that comes about through depth psychology allows us both to remedy our mistakes and to become more understanding and tolerant of others.

Self-knowledge can have a healing effect on ourselves and our environment, but this seldom happens without a prolonged period of professional analysis. Self-analysis works to the extent that we are alert to the effects of our behavior and willing to learn from them; however, it is limited by our blind-spots—our complexes—

---

81 Ibid., pars. 493ff.

and by the silence of others who for one reason or another indulge us. To really get a handle on ourselves we need an honest, objective mirror, which our intimates rarely are. The unconscious, in its many manifestations through dreams, visions, fantasies, accidents, active imagination and synchronicity, is a rather more unsparing mirror, and analysts are trained to interpret the reflections.

Again and again, patients dream of analytic work as a refreshing and purifying bath. Symbols of rebirth frequently appear in their dreams. The knowledge of what is going on in their unconscious gives them renewed vitality.

There are many methods and techniques espoused by therapists of different schools, but Jung's view was that technique is not important. What matters is rather the analyst's own self-knowledge and continuing attention to his or her own unconscious. Analysis is in fact both a craft and an art. Whatever school an analyst trains in, he or she is obliged to deal in an individual way with what comes in the door. Jung said that when a unique, suffering person was in front of him, he put theory on the shelf and simply listened. Only after he had heard the conscious facts did he look for compensating messages from the unconscious.

Self-knowledge can be the antidote to acute depression or a pervasive malaise of unknown origin, both particularly common in middle age. And it can be a spur to an adventurous inner life—the heroic journey, as it may be called. Understanding oneself is a matter of asking the right questions, again and again, and experimenting with answers. Do that long enough and the capital-S Self, one's regulating center, is activated.

Marie-Louise von Franz says that having a relationship with the Self is like being in touch with an "instinct of truth"—an immediate awareness of what is right and true, a truth without reflection:

> One reacts rightly without knowing why, it flows through one and one does the right thing. . . . With the help of the instinct of truth, life goes on as a meaningful flow, as a manifestation of the Self.[82]

---

[82] *Alchemy: An Introduction to the Symbolism and the Psychology,* pp. 172f.

In terms of relationships and the vicissitudes of everyday life, this comes down to simply *knowing* what is right for oneself. One has a strong instinctive feeling of what should be and what could be. To depart from this leads to error, aberration and illness.

24
Personality and Aloneness

The development of personality . . . is at once a charisma and a curse, because its first fruit is the segregation of the single individual from the undifferentiated and unconscious herd. This means isolation, and there is no more comforting word for it. Neither family nor society nor position can save one from this fate, nor yet the most successful adaptation to the environment.[83]

Being alone is relatively easy for introverts. They may lack a vital, on-going connection with the outer world but they generally have an active inner life. Extraverts are used to hustle and bustle and find it more difficult to live with just themselves. But whatever one's typology, the great challenge in the development of personality is to find a personal center. Elsewhere in this book I have spoken of the need for a personal container, but they come to the same thing.

Initially one's center is projected onto the immediate family, a self-contained unit experienced as wholeness. Without a family, whether nurturing or repressive, we are apt to feel rootless, at loose ends. The loss of such a container is clearly at work behind the emotional distress of orphans or a child whose parents split up, but that same motif is also constellated in grown-ups when one ascribes to values other than those sanctioned by the collective, or when any close relationship breaks up.

Loneliness feels like one has been abandoned. Mythologically, abandonment is associated with the childhood experience of gods and divine heroes—Zeus, Dionysus, Poseidon, Moses, Romulus and Remus, and so on. In fact, the motif is so widespread that Jung describes abandonment as "a necessary condition and not just a concomitant symptom," of the potentially higher consciousness

[83] "The Development of Personality," *The Development of Personality,* CW 17, pars. 293f.

symbolized by images of the child in a person's dreams.[84]

Anyone in the process of becoming independent must detach from his or her origins: mother, family, society. Sometimes this transition happens smoothly. If it does not, the result is twofold: the "poor me" syndrome, characteristic of the regressive longing for dependence, and a psychic experience of a potentially creative nature—the positive side of the divine child archetype: new life, exciting new possibilities. The incompatibility between these two directions generates a conflict that may precipitate a psychological crisis. The conflict is the price that has to be paid in order to grow up. On the one hand, we long to return to the past; on the other, we are drawn inexorably toward an unknown future.

Initially, this conflict goes hand in hand with the feeling of loneliness, behind which is the archetypal motif of the abandoned child. Thus Jung observes, "Higher consciousness . . . is equivalent to being *all alone in the world.*"[85] In short, individuation and personality are gifts that are paid for dearly.

The antidote to the feeling of loneliness, of abandonment, is the development of personality. But this does not happen unless one chooses his or her own way consciously and with moral deliberation. And you can make a commitment to go your own way only if you believe that way to be better for you than conventional ways of a moral, social, political or religious nature—any of the well-known "isms." Those who adhere to them do not choose their own way; they develop not themselves but a method and a collective mode of life at the cost of their own wholeness.

Personality is not the prerogative of genius, nor is mental prowess a significant factor in individuation. Just as in fairy tales, where so many psychic patterns are illustrated, the one who finds the treasure "hard to attain" is as often as not a Dummling, an innocent fool who simply follows his instincts.

---

[84] "The Psychology of the Child Archetype," *The Archetypes and the Collective Unconscious,* CW 9i, par. 287.

[85] Ibid., par. 288.

25
The Religious Attitude and Soul-Making

Among all my patients in the second half of life—that is to say, over thirty-five—there has not been one whose problem in the last resort was not that of finding a religious outlook on life.[86]

There are those who misunderstand Jungian psychology to be a religion, and for that reason either worship it as a fount of knowledge or decry it as the devil's own work. Jung himself denied that his school of analytical psychology was a religious movement:

> I am speaking just as a philosopher. People sometimes call me a religious leader. I am not that. I have no messages, no mission. I attempt only to understand. We are philosophers in the old sense of the word, lovers of wisdom. That avoids the sometimes questionable company of those who offer a religion.[87]

On the other hand, Jung did believe that the human longing for consciousness is essentially a religious activity. For instance, in an essay identifying five prominent instincts—creativity, reflection, activity, sexuality and hunger—he included the religious urge as a subset of reflection.[88]

Jung, himself a Swiss Protestant pastor's son who decried his father's mindless faith,[89] stressed that when he spoke of religion, or "the religious urge," he was not referring to belief in a particular creed or membership of a church, but rather to a certain attitude of mind. He described this attitude in terms of the Latin word *religio,* from *relegere,* meaning a careful consideration and observation of irrational factors historically conceived as spirits, demons, gods,

[86] "Psychotherapists or the Clergy," *Psychology and Religion,* CW 11, par. 509.
[87] *C.G. Jung Speaking,* p. 98.
[88] "Psychological Factors in Human Behaviour," *The Structure and Dynamics of the Psyche,* CW 8, pars. 235ff.
[89] See *Memories, Dreams, Reflections,* pp. 92ff.

goblins and horrors under the bed—"the attitude peculiar to a consciousness which has been changed by experience of the *numinosum*"[90]—which is to say, the unknown.

Thus someone in a conflict situation, he said, has to rely on

> divine comfort and mediation . . . . an autonomous psychic happening, a hush that follows the storm, a reconciling light in the darkness . . . secretly bringing order into the chaos of his soul.[91]

Although Jung often used the word "soul" in its traditional theological sense, he strictly limited its psychological meaning. "By soul," he writes, "I understand a clearly demarcated functional complex that can best be described as 'personality.' "[92] Thus soul-making, in this secular sense, can be seen as a natural consequence of differentiating and assimilating previously unconscious contents, particularly shadow and anima/animus.

Personally, I experience soul when I stare at the wall in the still of the night. Soul is there when I am in conflict with myself, when I struggle for answers. Soul is what I am, as opposed to what I seem to be. Soul is forged in the interactions between me and my inner complexes (persona, shadow, anima, etc.), between me and my outer companions (friends, family, colleagues), and I see abundant evidence of it daily in my analytic practice.

At times of transition from one stage of life to another, traditional religious imagery often appears in dreams. A childless woman in her forties dreams of baptizing her new-born. A man in his fifties dreams of finding a long-lost baby boy under a pile of rubble in the basement of a church. People dream of being priests or nuns, of celebrating Mass, of family seders, of pilgrimages, of mountainous journeys, fearful descents into black holes, wandering in the desert. A shopping mall becomes a mosque. Shrines magically appear in parking lots. Virgin births and divine children—born walking and speaking—are not rare.

---

[90] "Psychology and Religion," *Psychology and Religion,* CW 11, par. 9.
[91] "A Psychological Approach to the Dogma of the Trinity," ibid., par. 260.
[92] "Definitions," *Psychological Types,* CW 6, par. 797.

The particular significance of such images is inextricably bound up with the dreamer's personal history and associations, but beyond that they seem to derive from a common bedrock, the archetypal basis for all mythology and all religion—the search for meaning. Hence Jung writes that a neurosis "must be understood, ultimately, as the suffering of a soul which has not discovered its meaning."[93]

Marie-Louise von Franz notes that Jung realized early in his life that institutionalized religion could give him no answers. Instead, he found the way to illumination in the depths of himself; thus:

> The basis and substance of Jung's entire life and work do not lie in the traditions and religions which have become contents of collective consciousness, but rather in that primordial experience which is the source of these contents: the encounter of the single individual with his own god or daimon, his struggle with the emotions, affects, fantasies and creative inspirations and obstacles which come to light from within.[94]

The religious attitude can hardly be pinned down in a sentence or two, but it certainly involves acknowledging, and paying homage to, something numinous, mysterious—something far greater than oneself. God? Nature? The Self? Take your pick.

Jungian analyst Lawrence Jaffe writes:

> Jung says of his message that it sounds like religion, but is not. He claims to be speaking as a philosopher, whereas on other occasions he rejected even that designation, preferring to be considered an empirical scientist. Consistently he rejected the idea that he was a religious leader—understandable in view of the usual fate of founders of new religions (like Christ): dismemberment and early death.
>
> Jung's protestations notwithstanding, his psychology can be considered a kind of religion; not a traditional religion with an emphasis on dogma, faith and ritual, to be sure, but a new kind—a religion of experience.[95]

---

93 "Psychotherapists or the Clergy," *Psychology and Religion,* CW 11, par. 497.

94 *C.G. Jung: His Myth in Our Time,* pp. 13f.

95 *Liberating the Heart: Spirituality and Jungian Psychology,* p. 19.

Well, I can live with that, for when all is said and done, what is the wellspring of religion if not humanity's age-old experience of the gods? Nowadays we may call them archetypes or complexes, but we might as well call them turnips. By any name they will always be essentially unknown. Jungian psychology locates these "gods" inside instead of out, but the alchemists saw little difference, according to this ancient Hermetic ditty quoted more than once by Jung himself:

> Heaven above,
> Heaven below.
> Stars above,
> Stars below.
> All that is above
> Also is below.
> Grasp this
> And rejoice.[96]

---

[96] See, for instance, "The Psychology of the Transference," *The Practice of Psychotherapy,* CW 16, par. 384.

26
The Puer/Puella Syndrome

The lovely apparition of the puer aeternus *is, alas,*
a form of illusion. In reality he is a parasite on the mother,
a creature of her imagination,
who only lives when rooted in the maternal body.[97]

The expression *puer aeternus* is Latin for "eternal boy." In Greek mythology it designates a child-god who is forever young, like Iacchus, Dionysus, Eros. The theme is immortalized in the modern classics *Peter Pan* and *The Picture of Dorian Gray.*

In Jungian psychology, the term "puer" is used to describe an adult man whose emotional life has remained at an adolescent level, usually coupled with too great a dependence on the mother. The term "puella" is used for a woman, though one also speaks of a woman with a puer animus—a father's daughter.[98] The puer/puella syndrome is not an issue in one's early years, because the symptoms then are age-appropriate, but many psychological crises in later life arise from the inner need to grow out of this stage.

The typical puer does not look his age and is proud of it. Who would not be, in a culture where youth is valued more than old age? Any man would be shocked at the suggestion that his youthful appearance derives from emotional immaturity; ditto women.

Here is how a modern novelist describes her experience of puers:

> Fay knew about men who wouldn't grow up, and she wished she could tell Lizzie [her daughter], warn her. But she knew Lizzie wouldn't listen any more than she had listened.
>
> A man like this is so wildly attractive, so maddeningly alive, that he is absolutely irresistible. In the Tarot deck, he is the Fool . . . .

---

[97] *Symbols of Transformation,* CW 5, par. 393.

[98] See Marion Woodman, *The Pregnant Virgin: A Process of Psychological Transformation,* esp. pp. 35ff.

> In the picture on the card, the Fool, like a hobo, carries a sack tied to a stick. They leave you, these men, but they never said they were staying, never said they were committed, or purposeful—or responsible, even. All they want is to have a good time. And what's wrong with that? Nothing, except you begin to wonder how interested *you* are in just having a good time. . . .
>
> The joy of being with these men is the giddy return, through them, to a child's world, where there are no clocks and no claims on your time, no clothes to be kept clean, and no consequences to be considered. Days and nights are filled with the silliness, the spontaneity, the conspiratorial privacy, and all the breathless secret pleasures of life in a tree house. . . .
>
> They don't always come home, and they won't even apologize for it. They won't help around the house because they like it all messed up. They won't work very hard because they don't want to get trapped by success. And they won't work at the relationship because it's not supposed to be work, it's supposed to be fun. If you don't want to play with them, they don't mind. But that isn't going to stop them from playing.
>
> Somehow, they make you feel very old, these men. They turn you into their mother.[99]

Of course, not every woman finds such men "wildly attractive," much less irresistible. Why not? Well, following the natural "law" that we see in others traits of our own of which we are unconscious (the essence of projection), women who fall for puers are themselves quite likely to be puellas. And, as it happens, vice versa.

The typical puer shirks responsibility for his actions, and understandably so, since what he does is not within his conscious control. He is at the mercy of his unconscious, and is especially vulnerable to his instinctive drives. He is prone to do what "feels right." However, he is so alienated from his true feelings that what feels right one minute often feels wrong the next. Hence, for instance, he may find himself in erotic situations that cause him a good deal of distress the next day—or indeed that night, in his dreams.

---

[99] Marsha Norman, *The Fortune Teller,* pp. 116f.

The individuating puer—one coming to grips with his attitudes and behavior patterns—knows that undifferentiated feelings are highly suspect, especially when they arise in conjunction with the use of alcohol or other drugs. Instead of identifying with his feelings, he tries to keep some distance from them, which means objectifying what he is experiencing. He questions himself: Is this what I really feel? Is this what I want? What are the consequences? Can I live with them? Can I live with myself? How does what I do affect others?

Puers generally have a hard time with commitment. They like to keep their options open and can't bear to be tied down. They act spontaneously, with little thought of consequences. The individuating puer has to sacrifice this rather charming trait—but what he sacrifices then becomes part of his shadow. In order then not to become an automaton, ruled by habit and routine, he will have to reassimilate—this time consciously—his lapsed puer characteristics.

Also symptomatic of puer psychology is the feeling of being special, of having a unique destiny. When you feel like that, it's hard to muster the energy to earn a living. Compared to what you're cut out for, the daily grind is just too mundane. This is a variety of inflation. You feel special, so why, you ask yourself, am I doing something so ordinary?

If this attitude persists, you can cheerfully rationalize wasting your life, waiting for destiny to catch up—or fall from the sky. You play the lotteries and buy stocks. You know the odds are against you but you cross your fingers and hope you'll win, and you hedge your bets with options and silver futures.

Puers and puellas live a provisional life. There is always the fear of being caught in a situation from which it might not be possible to escape. Their lot is seldom what they really want; they are always "about to" do something, to make a change; one day they will do what is necessary—but not just yet. They are awash in a world of "maybe": "Maybe I'll do this . . . maybe I'll do that . . ." Plans for the future come to nothing; life slips away in fantasies of what will be, what could be, while no decisive action is taken to change the here and now.

The provisional life is a kind of prison. The bars are the parental complexes, unconscious ties to early life, the boundless irresponsibility of the child. Thus the dreams of puers and puellas are full of prison imagery: chains, bars, cages, entrapment, bondage. Life itself, reality as they find it, is experienced as imprisonment. They yearn for independence and long for freedom, but they are powerless to pull it off.

Puers chafe at boundaries and limits and tend to view any restriction as intolerable. They do not realize that some restrictions are indispensable for growth. This is expressed in the *I Ching,* the Chinese book of wisdom, as follows:

> Unlimited possibilities are not suited to man; if they existed, his life would only dissolve in the boundless. To become strong, a man's life needs the limitations ordained by duty and voluntarily accepted. The individual attains significance as a free spirit only by surrounding himself with these limitations and by determining for himself what his duty is.[100]

Indeed, it is a lucky puer or puella whose unconscious eventually rebels and makes its dissatisfaction apparent through a psychological crisis. Otherwise you stay stuck and shallow.

The puer's opposite number, or shadow, is the *senex* (Latin, "old man"): disciplined, conscientious, organized. Similarly, the shadow of the senex is the puer: unbounded instinct, disordered, intoxicated, whimsical. The puer's mythological counterpart is the Greek god Dionysus, whose frenzied female followers—puella acolytes, so to speak—ripped men to pieces. Senex psychology is appropriately characterized by Saturn and the god Apollo: staid, rational, responsible.

It is said that the passage of time turns liberals into conservatives. Likewise, puers and puellas become old men and women, and, if they have learned from their experience, possibly even wise.

---

[100] Hexagram 60, "Limitation," in Richard Wilhelm, trans., *The I Ching or Book of Changes.*

But at any stage of life one must make a place for both puer and senex. In fact, whoever lives one pattern exclusively risks constellating the opposite. Enantiodromia is waiting in the wings: the more one-sided we are, the more likely it is that the opposite will break through to spin our lives around.

A healthy, well-balanced personality is capable of functioning according to what is appropriate at the time. That is the ideal, seldom attained without conscious effort and a psychological crisis. Hence analysis quite as often involves the need for a well-controlled person to reconnect with the spontaneous, instinctual life as it does the puella's or puer's need to grow up.

27
Working on Yourself

The goal is important only as an idea:
the essential thing is the opus which leads to the goal;
that *is the goal of a lifetime.*[101]

In the process of analytic work, your best is not what you have to offer intellectually, nor is your worst. You are graded not on what is in your head or what is in your heart—both being fickle parameters—but rather on who you are compared to who you could be. And even then, not by your analyst, but by what you progressively know of yourself from your own "instinct of truth."[102]

There are a lot of dull hours in analysis when nothing seems to be happening. Of course there is the occasional Eureka! when the heavens part and for a time all is clear, but the lasting revelations, the enduring insights, generally come only after prolonged attention to the mundane. This is quite a shock to those who go into analysis seeking the divine.

Everyday life is the raw material of analysis. It is analogous to what the alchemists called the *prima materia,* the lead or base metal they strived to turn into gold by melting and running its vapors through flasks and retorts, a process of distillation similar to making strong liquor from wine. The alchemists' *distillatio* is akin psychologically to the process of discrimination: the differentiation of moods and fantasies, attitudes, feelings and thoughts, with close attention to the nitty-gritty detail of conflict in relationships—the "he said," "she said" encounters that in the moment bring you to a boil and make you cringe when you cool down.

---

[101] "The Psychology of the Transference," *The Practice of Psychotherapy,* CW 16, par. 400.
[102] See above, pp. 91f.

All this, the base metal of your miserable life, you write down in a journal. That takes some discipline, but if you don't write it down you don't remember. Of course you can't record everything. You'd get lost in the forest and miss the trees. You note the highlights, particularly emotional reactions—because they signal the activation of complexes—and your conscious attitude toward them. You reflect on all this, mull it over, and then take it to your analyst.

Time is a big factor in this process. An hour or two a week with an analyst is never enough, but when it's all you've got you soon get used to it. In any case, the real work is what you do on your own between sessions; and if you don't do much on your own, then very little happens.

I think of Rilke's description of his neighbor, a Russian bureaucrat named Nikolai Kusmitch.

> Time was precious to Nikolai Kusmitch. He spent his days hoarding it, saving a second here, a minute or two there, sometimes a whole half hour. He imagined that the time he saved could be used to better advantage when he wasn't so busy. Perhaps it could even be tacked on at the end of his life, so he'd live longer.
>
> He sought out what he thought must certainly exist: a state institution for time, a kind of Time Bank you could make deposits in and then draw on. He didn't find one, so he kept the loose change in his head.
>
> Nikolai Kusmitch did what he could to economize, but after a few weeks it struck him that he was still spending too much.
>
> "I must retrench," he thought.
>
> He rose earlier. He washed less thoroughly. He dressed quickly, ate his toast standing up and drank coffee on the run. But on Sundays, when he came to settle his accounts, he always found that nothing remained of his savings.
>
> In the end, Nikolai Kusmitch died as he had lived, a pauper.[103]

Working on yourself is something like that. You can't save it up for Sundays; it's what you do during the week that counts.

---

[103] *The Notebook of Malte Laurids Brigge*, pp. 161ff. (modified).

28
Bringing Fantasies into Life

Continual conscious realization of unconscious fantasies, together with active participation in the fantastic events, has . . . the effect firstly of extending the conscious horizon by the inclusion of numerous unconscious contents; secondly of gradually diminishing the dominant influence of the unconscious; and thirdly of bringing about a change of personality.[104]

Becoming conscious of one's fantasies, otherwise known as active imagination, is a useful activity for tracking what is going on the unconscious. It is not generally recommended for those not in analysis because what comes up may not have a pretty face and can in fact be quite scary. Also, perhaps fortunately, active imagination is not easy to get into.

Active imagination can involve painting, writing, music, dance, working in clay or stone—whatever you feel like doing. You follow your energy where it wants to go. The less formal training you have the better, because the trained mind inhibits freedom of expression. It is a way of giving the unconscious an outlet, so you don't explode. It is also another kind of container; instead of dumping your affect on other people you keep it to yourself—you take responsibility for what's yours.

Speaking for myself, I was unable to do active imagination until a friend suggested some simple steps. The first of these was aimed at overcoming my fear of a blank sheet of paper.

"Take a page of a newspaper," he said. "Lay a plate on it. Draw an outline of the plate with a crayon or a colored pencil or a paint brush. Look at what you made. Think about it. Now do something

[104] "The Technique of Differentiation," *Two Essays on Analytical Psychology,* CW 7, par. 358.

inside the circle. You can do anything you want—anything! It's all up to you."

This was wily advice because, as I later learned, any circular image is in effect a mandala, and mandalas are traditionally, that is to say archetypally, containers of the mystery. At the time I certainly needed a container, and everything was a mystery to me.

Before long my walls were covered with images of my inner life: gaudy mandalas, stick figures, fanciful doodles, depictions of a mood. I graduated from newspaper to cardboard to good quality bond. I used whatever came to hand: pencils, pen, paint, felt-tipped markers, fingers, toes, my tongue! All crude reflections of whatever was going on in me when I did them. They had no style or technique and people who came to visit my hole-in-the-wall apartment looked askance. When I come across them now they do seem grotesque, but at the time I loved them and my soul rejoiced.

Jung himself pioneered active imagination by painting and writing his dreams and fantasies, and some he chiseled in stone. In fact, he pinpointed this work on himself as fundamental both to his formulation of the anima/animus concept and to the importance of personifying unconscious contents:

> When I was writing down these fantasies, I once asked myself, "What am I really doing? Certainly this has nothing to do with science. But then what is it?" Whereupon a voice within said, "It is art." I was astonished. It had never entered my head that what I was writing had any connection with art. Then I thought, "Perhaps my unconscious is forming a personality that is not me, but which is insisting on coming through to expression." I knew for a certainty that the voice had come from a woman.[105]

Jung said very emphatically to this voice that his fantasies had nothing to do with art, and he felt a great inner resistance.

> Then came the next assault, and again the same assertion: "That is art." This time I caught her and said, "No, it is not art! On the contrary, it is nature," and prepared myself for an argument. When

[105] *Memories, Dreams, Reflections,* pp. 210f.

> nothing of the sort occurred, I reflected that the "woman within me" did not have the speech centres I had. And so I suggested that she use mine. She did so and came through with a long statement.

Intrigued by the fact that a woman could interfere with him from within, Jung concluded that she must be his "soul," in the primitive sense of the word, traditionally thought of as feminine.

> I came to see that this inner feminine figure plays a typical, or archetypical, role in the unconscious of a man . . . . I called her the "anima." The corresponding figure in a woman I called the "animus."

Jung also realized that by personifying that inner voice he was less likely to be seduced into believing he was something he wasn't (i.e., an artist). In effect, he was writing letters to his anima, a part of himself with a viewpoint different from his conscious one. And by writing out, or sculpting, his fantasies, he gave her no chance "to twist them into intrigues":

> If I had taken these fantasies of the unconscious as art, they would have carried no more conviction than visual perceptions, as if I were watching a movie. I would have felt no moral obligation towards them. The anima might then have easily seduced me into believing that I was a misunderstood artist, and that my so-called artistic nature gave me the right to neglect reality. If I had followed her voice, she would in all probability have said to me one day, "Do you imagine the nonsense you're engaged in is really art? Not a bit."[106]

The object of active imagination, then, is to give a voice to sides of the personality one is ordinarily not aware of—to establish a line of communication between consciousness and the unconscious. It is not necessary to interpret what the material "means." You do it and you live with it. Something goes on between you and what you create, and it doesn't need to be put into words to be effective.

---

[106] Ibid.

29
More on Fantasies

A fantasy needs to be understood both causally and purposively. Causally interpreted, it seems like a symptom of a physiological state, the outcome of antecedent events. Purposively interpreted, it seems like a symbol, seeking to characterize a definite goal with the help of the material at hand, or trace out a line of future psychological development.[107]

In my own analytic process, once I started painting and drawing, I stopped feeling sorry for myself. I also stopped suspecting that my loved one was up to hanky-panky when I wasn't around. I focused on myself and how I felt. Whenever I got into a mood, I captured it with a concrete image or had a talk with my inner woman. Instead of accusing others of causing my heartache, I asked my heart why it ached. Then I drew or wrote an answer.

One of my early paintings showed a man with head bent, under a black cloud. A bird fluttered above him.

"What kind of bird is that?" asked my analyst.

I considered. "A raven comes to mind."

"In alchemy," he said, "the raven is a symbol for the *nigredo*—melancholy, an affliction of the soul, confusion, depression."

That took me to a mournful passage in Franz Kafka's *Diaries,* which had been my personal bible for some fifteen years. In the next session I read it to my analyst:

> I don't believe people exist whose inner plight resembles mine; still, it is possible for me to imagine such people—but that the secret raven forever flaps about their heads as it does about mine, even to imagine that is impossible.[108]

---

[107] "Definitions," *Psychological Types,* CW 6, par. 720.
[108] *The Diaries of Franz Kafka, 1914-1923,* p. 195.

"Yes, the 'poor me' syndrome," he nodded, "heavily laced with inflation, the feeling of being special—nobody suffers as much as you do. As if depression played favorites."

I swallowed that and worked on it.

Every time I went to analysis I took something new. Once I made a pair of clay penises. One was tiny, a shriveled little thing; the other was erect and powerful. We set them up between us.

"David and Goliath?" said my analyst.

"Bud Abbott and Lou Costello?" I suggested. "Mutt and Jeff?"

One of my first sketches showed a woman tied to a rock. Right away I tagged it as the feminine fused with matter, which I knew related symbolically to the Eve stage of anima development—being mother-bound. I described it to my analyst as my mountain-anima because it reminded me of fairy tales where the princess is imprisoned on top of a mountain.

"A real sweetheart," he observed. "But she has no feet."

I took this to mean that my feelings weren't grounded, and I worked on that too.

Writing is for many the most satisfying form of active imagination. You have a dialogue with what's going on inside. You conjure up an image of what you're feeling, personify it and talk to it, then you listen to what it says back. You write this down to make it real, to give it substance. That's the difference between active imagination and a daydream. If you don't fix it in time and space, it's pie in the sky.

Active imagination can also take the form of dreaming a dream on—you pick up the action at the end of a dream and imagine what might happen next. This is a good way to learn more about your complexes, but to do it successfully you have to still your skeptical, rational mind, which will call it nonsense and say you made it all up. And of course you did—but who is "you"? Nonsense it may seem, but wisdom it may hold.

Jung emphasized that for active imagination to be psychologically useful, which is to say transformative, one has to move beyond a merely aesthetic appreciation of the action or images and take an ethical stand toward them—relate them to what is happening in your life, and judge their meaning in that context:

> As a rule there is a marked tendency simply to enjoy this interior entertainment and to leave it at that. Then, of course, there is no real progress but only endless variations on the same theme, which is not the point of the exercise at all. . . . If the observer understands that his own drama is being performed on this inner stage, he cannot remain indifferent to the plot and its dénouement. He will notice, as the actors appear one by one and the plot thickens, that they all have some purposeful relationship to his conscious situation, that he is being addressed by the unconscious and that *it* causes these fantasy-images to appear before him.[109]

Recognizing your own involvement, you are then obliged to enter into the process with your personal reactions, just as if you were one of the fantasy figures—as if the drama being enacted were real. As indeed it is, for psychic facts are quite as real as table-tops. If you place yourself in the drama as you really are, not only does it gain in actuality but you also create, by your criticism of the fantasy, an effective counterbalance to its tendency to get out of hand.

---

[109] *Mysterium Coniunctionis,* CW 14, par. 706.

What you are experiencing, after all, is an encounter with the unconscious, the *sine qua non* of the transcendent function and another step on the path of individuation.

For those in analysis, active imagination of one kind or another is good preparation for leaving. You don't stay in therapy forever. When the time comes to stop, to be on your own, it is a useful tool to take away with you.

30
The Inner Voice

Anyone with a vocation hears the voice of the inner man: he is called.[110]

What is it, asks Jung, that induces one to rise out of unconscious identity with the mass as out of a swathing mist? He suggests that it is due to many and various irrational factors, but particularly to something commonly called vocation:

> True personality is always a vocation and puts its trust in it as in God, despite its being, as the ordinary man would say, only a personal feeling. But vocation acts like a law of God from which there is no escape. The fact that many a man who goes his own way ends in ruin means nothing to one who has a vocation. He *must* obey his own law, as if it were a daemon whispering to him of new and wonderful paths.[111]

Having a vocation originally meant "to be addressed by a voice." Examples of this are ubiquitous in the writings of the Old Testament prophets.

When I was in Zurich training to be an analyst I listened for that voice. Was analytic work truly my vocation? If the voice called, would I hear? What if it did not? Or, almost worse, what if it did? I was mindful of the way Samuel, as told in the Bible, became one of the elect:

> And it came to pass at that time . . . ere the lamp of God went out in the temple of the Lord, where the ark of God was, and Samuel was laid down to sleep;
>
> That the Lord called Samuel: and he answered, Here am I.

---

[110] "The Development of Personality," *The Development of Personality,* CW 17, par. 299.
[111] Ibid.

> And he ran unto Eli, and said, Here am I; for thou calledst me. And he said, I called not; lie down again. . . .
>
> And the Lord called yet again, Samuel. And Samuel arose and went to Eli, and said, Here am I; for thou didst call me. And he answered, I called not, my son; lie down again. . . .
>
> And the Lord called Samuel again the third time. And he arose and went to Eli, and said, Here am I; for thou didst call me. And Eli perceived that the Lord had called the child.
>
> Therefore Eli said unto Samuel, Go, lie down: and it shall be, if he call thee, that thou shalt say, Speak, Lord; for thy servant heareth. So Samuel went and lay down in his place.
>
> And the Lord came, and stood, and called as at other times, Samuel, Samuel. Then Samuel answered, Speak; for thy servant heareth.[112]

That's more or less what happened to me. One night I distinctly heard my name called, not once but thrice, and then again.

"Speak!" I cried, leaping out of bed, "I do heareth!"

I was ripe for holy orders before I heard my housemate Arnold snickering behind the door. We had a good old pillow fight then. Puers at heart. But having already accepted that God—a.k.a. the Self—moves in mysterious ways, it was not a great leap of faith to imagine my feckless friend as His unwitting messenger. Jung:

> Vocation, or the feeling of it, is not, however, the prerogative of great personalities; it is also appropriate to the small ones all the way down to the "midget" personalities, but as the size decreases the voice becomes more and more muffled and unconscious. It is as if the voice of the daemon within were moving further and further off, and spoke more rarely and more indistinctly. The smaller the personality, the dimmer and more unconscious it becomes, until finally it merges indistinguishably with the surrounding society, thus surrendering its own wholeness and dissolving into the wholeness of the group.[113]

---

112 1 Sam. 3: 2-10, Authorized Version.

113 "The Development of Personality," *The Development of Personality*, CW 17, par. 302.

The "wholeness of the group" sounds like an oxymoron, but it is not; it simply designates our original state of unconsciousness, the *participation mystique* that we all wallow in before we have differentiated ourselves from the collective.

Differentiation is necessary because the call to become whole is not heard en masse. In any group the inner voice is drowned out by convention, and one's personal vocation is overwhelmed by collective necessity.

The primary question in speaking of vocation is always, "Do you know who you are? Are you living your own way?"

Caveat: In modern times, Goethe and Napoleon heeded inner voices that fueled their sense of personal destiny. So did Hitler and Stalin, and so do many others diagnosed as psychotic, which just goes to show that inner voices aren't necessarily benign. Their interpretation depends on a discriminating consciousness in those who hear them.

31
Group Work

Even a small group is ruled by a suggestive group spirit which, when it is good, can have very favourable effects, although at the cost of spiritual and moral independence of the individual.[114]

Doing psychological work in groups becomes ever more popular. In the sixties and seventies, there were so-called encounter groups and not much else. Nowadays there is group therapy for everything and everyone, from victims of abuse to abusers, from addicts and their partners to reformed dope dealers, from those seeking collective solace for lost foreskin to those who feel guilty about eating over sinks. Clearly many people find real value in sharing their traumatic or deviant experiences. That is abreaction; it is cathartic and it has a place. However, it is a far remove from what is involved in the process of individuation. Jung:

> The group enhances the ego . . . but the self is diminished and put in the background in favour of the average. . . . Instead of finding security and independence in oneself, which is what is needed, the danger exists that the individual will make the group into a father and mother and therefore remain as dependent, insecure and infantile as before.[115]

This is not to deny the widespread desire to change and the genuine search for a transformative experience. But a temporarily heightened awareness does not equal rebirth. You may think you have been forever changed when you are merely inflated with an overdose of previously unconscious material. Many is the analysand who has come to me high as a kite after a weekend workshop and had to be peeled off the ceiling.

---

[114] Jung correspondence, quoted in von Franz, *C.G. Jung*, p. 262.
[115] Ibid.

Jung acknowledged that one can feel transformed during a group experience, but he cautioned against confusing this with the real thing. He pointed out that the presence of many people together exerts great suggestive force due to the phenomenon of *participation mystique,* unconscious identification; hence in a crowd one risks becoming the victim of one's own suggestibility. Jung writes:

> If any considerable group of persons are united and identified with one another by a particular frame of mind, the resultant transformation experience bears only a very remote resemblance to the experience of individual transformation. A group experience takes place on a lower level of consciousness than the experience of an individual. This is due to the fact that, when many people gather together to share one common emotion, the total psyche emerging from the group is below the level of the individual psyche. If it is a very large group, the collective psyche will be more like the psyche of an animal, which is the reason why the ethical attitude of large organizations is always doubtful. The psychology of a large crowd inevitably sinks to the level of mob psychology. . . . In the crowd one feels no responsibility, but also no fear.[116]

Positive group experiences are certainly possible. They can spur a person to noble deeds or instill a feeling of solidarity with others. The group can give one a degree of courage, a bearing and dignity that may easily get lost in isolation. But in the long run such gifts are unearned and so do not last. Away from the crowd and alone, you are a different person and unable to reproduce the previous state of mind.

For some people, dealing with what happens to them in the course of an ordinary day is either too difficult or too mundane, sometimes both. Esoteric group practices—crystal balls, vision quests, pendulums, channeling and the like—are much more exciting. They tempt with promises few are immune to: deliverance from the woes of this world and escape from oneself.

---

[116] "Concerning Rebirth," *The Archetypes and the Collective Unconscious,* CW 9i, par. 225.

This has been as true for me as for anyone else. Before I went into Jungian analysis I sought enlightenment in the study of astrology, graphology, palmistry, phrenology (bumps on the skull), Rosicrucianism, yoga, existentialism and more—all very interesting, indeed, but when it came to the crunch—when I found myself on my knees—they were no help at all.

To my mind, and in my experience, group work can be valuable in terms of individuation only if one's experience in the group is viewed as grist for the mill of personal analysis, which is where all our wayward chickens come home to roost.

32
The Inflated Ego

An inflated consciousness is always egocentric and conscious of nothing but its own existence.[117]

Hearing the call is a numinous experience. Such events always have a deep emotional resonance. Hitherto unconscious contents have become conscious. What was previously unknown is now known. That automatically results in an enlargement of the personality. Cults, sudden "born again" conversions and other far-reaching changes of mind—like Paul on the road to Damascus—have their origin in such experiences. Whether for good or ill, only time will tell. Consciousness is temporarily disoriented, life as one has known it is disrupted, and when the ego is particularly weak the entire personality may disintegrate.

The extreme possibility is schizophrenia, a splitting of the mind—multiple personalities with no central control, a free-for-all among the complexes. But the more common danger is inflation, an unavoidable concomitant of realizing new things about oneself.

Inflation is a psychological phenomenon that involves an extension of the personality beyond individual limits. This regularly happens in analysis, as ego-awareness lights up the dark, but it is common in everyday life as well. One example is the way in which people identify with their business or title, as if they themselves were the whole complex of social factors which in fact characterize only their position. This is an unwarranted extension of oneself, whimsically bestowed by others.

Here are two passages by Jung on inflation:

> "Knowledge puffeth up," Paul writes to the Corinthians, for the new knowledge had turned the heads of many, as indeed constantly hap-

[117] *Psychology and Alchemy,* CW 12, par. 563.

> pens. The inflation has nothing to do with the *kind* of knowledge, but simply and solely with the fact that any new knowledge can so seize hold of a weak head that he no longer sees and hears anything else. He is hypnotized by it, and instantly believes he has solved the riddle of the universe. But that is equivalent to almighty self-conceit.[118]

> An inflated consciousness is . . . . incapable of learning from the past, incapable of understanding contemporary events, and incapable of drawing right conclusions about the future. It is hypnotized by itself and therefore cannot be argued with. It inevitably dooms itself to calamities that must strike it dead. Paradoxically enough, inflation is a regression of consciousness into unconsciousness. This always happens when consciousness takes too many unconscious contents upon itself and loses the faculty of discrimination, the *sine qua non* of all consciousness.[119]

Every step toward greater consciousness creates a kind of Promethean guilt. Through self-knowledge, the gods are, as it were, robbed of their fire; that is, something that was the property of unconscious powers is torn out of its natural context and subordinated to the whims of the conscious mind. The one who has "stolen" the new knowledge becomes alienated from others. The pain of this loneliness is the vengeance of the gods, for never again can one return to the fold. Prometheus's punishment was to be chained to the lonely cliffs of the Caucasus, forsaken of God and man. An eagle fed on his liver, and as much as was devoured during the day, that much grew again during the night.

Fortunately, few of us have to go through all that. The ancient notion of the liver as the seat of the soul may linger on, but nowadays common sense and the reactions of others to an assumed god-likeness are usually enough to bring one down to earth.

However, there is still the feeling of having been chosen, set apart. Thus anyone who has found his or her individual path is

---

[118] "The Relations Between the Ego and the Unconscious," *Two Essays on Analytical Psychology,* CW 7, par. 243, note 1.
[119] *Psychology and Alchemy,* CW 12, par. 563.

bound to feel estranged from those who have not. This is simply a particular case of what I have generally observed, that those who have worked on themselves don't care to spend much time with those who haven't. One might think this to be elitist, but it is only natural. With a sense of vocation comes the realization that your time on this earth is precious. You become reluctant to squander it on those who don't know who they are or why they are here, and are not inclined to ask.

Those who hear the call and respond become redeemer personalities—leaders, heroes, beacons of hope for others. Individuals with personality have *mana*.[120]

But beware of those who seek vaingloriously to capitalize on this aura, including yourself. Those with *mana* may seem to be in possession of an absolute truth, but in fact the main thing they have that distinguishes them from others is a bedrock sense of themselves and the resolve to obey the law that commands from within.

---

[120] *Mana* is a Melanesian word referring to a bewitching or numinous quality in gods and sacred objects. In individual psychology, Jung used the term "mana personality" to describe the inflationary result of assimilating previously unconscious contents.

Bibliography

Campbell, Joseph. *Hero with a Thousand Faces* (Bollingen Series XVII). Princeton: Princeton University Press, 1949.

Jaffe, Lawrence W. *Liberating the Heart: Spirituality and Jungian Psychology.* Toronto: Inner City Books, 1990.

Jung, C.G. *The Collected Works* (Bollingen Series XX). 20 vols. Trans. R.F.C. Hull. Ed. H. Read, M. Fordham, G. Adler, Wm. McGuire. Princeton: Princeton University Press, 1953-1979.

_______. *Man and His Symbols.* London: Aldus Books, 1964.

_______. *Memories, Dreams, Reflections.* Ed. Aniela Jaffé. New York: Pantheon Books, 1961.

_______. *The Psychology of Kundalini Yoga* (Bollingen Series XCIX). Ed. Sonu Shamdasani. Princeton: Princeton University Press, 1996.

_______. *Seminar 1925.* Mimeographed Notes. Zurich: C.G. Jung Institute, n.d.

_______. *The Visions Seminars, 1930-1934.* Zürich: Spring Publications, 1976.

Kafka, Franz. *The Diaries of Franz Kafka, 1914-1923.* Trans. Martin Greenberg. Ed. Max Brod. London: Secker and Warburg, 1949.

McGuire, William, ed. *The Freud/Jung* Letters (Bollingen Series XCIV). Trans. Ralph Manheim and R.F.C. Hull. Princeton: Princeton University Press, 1974.

Norman, Marsha. *The Fortune Teller.* New York: Bantam Books, 1988.

Plato. *The Symposium.* Trans. W.R.M. Lamb. Loeb Classical Library. Cambridge, MA: Harvard University Press, 1961.

Rilke, Rainer Maria. *The Notebook of Malte Laurids Brigge.* Trans. John Linton. London: The Hogarth Press, 1959.

Sharp, Daryl. *Getting To Know You: The Inside Out of Relationship.* Toronto: Inner City Books, 1992.

_______. *Who Am I, Really? Personality, Soul and Individuation.* Toronto: Inner City Books, 1995.

von Franz, Marie-Louise. *Alchemy: An Introduction to the Symbolism and the Psychology.* Toronto: Inner City Books, 1980.

_______. *C.G. Jung: His Myth in Our Time.* Trans. William H. Kennedy. 2nd ed. Toronto: Inner City Books, 1998.

_______. *Redemption Motifs in Fairytales.* Toronto: Inner City Books, 1980.

Wilhelm, Richard, trans. *The I Ching or Book of Changes.* London: Routledge and Kegan Paul, 1968.

Woodman, Marion. *The Pregnant Virgin: A Process of Psychological Transformation.* Toronto: Inner City Books, 1985.

Index

Also by Daryl Sharp in this Series

Prices and Payment in $US (except in Canada, $Cdn)

THE SECRET RAVEN
Conflict and Transformation in the Life of Franz Kafka
ISBN 0-919123-00-7. (1980) 128 pp. $16

PERSONALITY TYPES: Jung's Model of Typology
ISBN 0-919123-30-9. (1987) 128 pp. **Diagrams** $16

THE SURVIVAL PAPERS: Anatomy of a Midlife Crisis
ISBN 0-919123-34-1. (1988) 160 pp. $16

DEAR GLADYS: The Survival Papers, Book 2
ISBN 0-919123-36-8. (1989) 144 pp. $16

JUNG LEXICON: A Primer of Terms and Concepts
ISBN 0-919123-48-1. (1991) 160 pp. **Diagrams** $16

GETTING TO KNOW YOU: The Inside Out of Relationship
ISBN 0-919123-56-2. (1992) 128 pp. $16

THE BRILLIG TRILOGY:

> **1. CHICKEN LITTLE: The Inside Story** ***(A Jungian Romance)***
> ISBN 0-919123-62-7. (1993) 128 pp. $16
>
> **2. WHO AM I, REALLY? Personality, Soul and Individuation**
> ISBN 0-919123-68-6. (1995) 144 pp. $16
>
> **3. LIVING JUNG: The Good and the Better**
> ISBN 0-919123-73-2. (1996) 128 pp. $16

JUNGIAN PSYCHOLOGY UNPLUGGED
My Life As an Elephant
ISBN 0-919123-81-3. (1998) 160 pp. $16

CUMULATIVE INDEX of Inner City Books
The First 80 Titles, 1980-1998
ISBN 0-919123-82-1. (1999) 160 pp. **8-1/2" x 11"** $20

Discounts: any 3-5 books, 10%; 6-9 books, 20%; 10 or more, 25%
Add Postage/Handling: 1-2 books, $3 surface ($6 air); 3-4 books, $5 surface ($10 air); 5-9 books, $10 surface ($15 air); 10 or more, free surface ($20 air)

Ask for **Jung at Heart** newsletter and free Catalogue of **over 90 titles**

INNER CITY BOOKS
Box 1271, Station Q, Toronto, ON M4T 2P4, Canada
Tel. (416) 927-0355 / Fax (416) 924-1814 / E-mail: sales@innercitybooks.net